· A HISTORY LOVER'S ·
GUIDE TO
DALLAS

• A HISTORY LOVER'S •
GUIDE TO
DALLAS

GEORGETTE DRISCOLL | *Foreword by Mark Doty*

THE
History
PRESS

Published by The History Press
Charleston, SC
www.historypress.net

First published 2019

ISBN 9781540240538

Library of Congress Control Number: 2019943350

Notice: The information in this book is true and complete to the best of our knowledge. It is offered without guarantee on the part of the author or The History Press. The author and The History Press disclaim all liability in connection with the use of this book.

Every effort has been made by the author to make this guide as helpful and accurate as possible. Please keep in mind that many things can change after publishing, and it is always best to call before an outing to confirm the information and details included in this guide.

About the cover

Front cover, top: The Big D experienced many booms over the years. One of the most dramatic was the downtown building boom in the 1950s, which introduced many of the iconic skyscrapers still standing today. *Photograph by the author; bottom (left to right)*: Much like during the 1930s, when downtown had more than three hundred streetcars in operation, the M-Line trolley offers free rides through uptown, downtown and the Dallas Arts District. *Photograph by the author;* The Hall of State building at Fair Park now houses the Dallas Historical Society, which formed in 1922. The *Tejas Warrior* statue focuses attention toward the building's grand entrance. *Photograph by the author;* The City of Dallas manages almost four hundred parks containing over twenty thousand acres of land. Pictured are the swans at Fair Park, home of the State Fair of Texas. *Photograph by the author.*

Back cover: Located just northeast of Dallas, Farmers Branch was home to many of the first settlers in the Peters Colony. Original buildings and reconstructions can be explored at the Historical Park in Farmers Branch. *Photograph by the author; inset*: A flag at half-mast and flowers on the grassy knoll following the assassination of President John F. Kennedy on November 22, 1963. *Courtesy of Dallas Municipal Archives.*

CONTENTS

PREFACE

I was born and raised in New Mexico. My youth was spent amongst four-hundred-year-old low-slung adobe buildings in Santa Fe. The town was and still is very small, with a vibrant arts culture. I would safely ride my bike through the downtown square, where Native Americans sold jewelry made of turquois and silver. Along my route through the plaza, I'd pass the tallest building I knew, the Cathedral Basilica of St. Francis of Assisi.

Santa Fe has legislation that helps preserve the city's history, including ordinances that regulate the architecture style and building height. My family took day trips to Albuquerque, but that was the most exposure I had to a larger city. I was eight years old when my family took our first major road trip out of the Land of Enchantment.

It was evening before we made it to Dallas. My older sister and I were both sleeping soundly in the backseat. Our mom shook us awake to see the city. I wiped away the sleep and was absolutely in awe of what I saw. The glass skyscrapers, massive highways and busy people everywhere. Dallas was so new, so alive and so big.

At some point, I whispered to my sister that someday I would live in Dallas and work in one of those tall buildings. Some twenty-plus years later, I fulfilled that dream and moved to Dallas, working on the seventeenth floor of one of the skyscrapers that mesmerized me as a child.

Dallas was big to me as a child and is still big to me now. No wonder it's nicknamed the Big D. It lives up to the name, but not just because of the tall buildings and ever-expanding boundaries. It has a big history with big stories and big characters.

As my family settled in and started to explore Dallas, I pleasured in learning all I could about the history. I'm honored to share this with you in *A History Lover's Guide to Dallas*. The book starts with four chapters that focus on Dallas's past and feature sites that are relevant to the city's development. The following four chapters focus on specific visitor options related to art, music and theater, nature and sports. The book closes with resources and suggestions organized by area and season to further help readers plan their adventures.

Growing up in Santa Fe helped teach me the importance of history. The story of the Big D, as you will soon read, has been one of fast growth. I hope this book serves as an inspiration to slow down, learn from the past, help preserve historic places for the future and strive for equality for all.

Thank you to Mark Doty, chief planner and historic preservation officer for the City of Dallas and author of *Lost Dallas*, whose work tirelessly promotes preservation efforts and quality of life in Dallas. I am deeply grateful for the guidance and support provided by Ben Gibson and Sara Miller from The History Press. Thank you to Donna Kidby, whose take on life is always refreshing and who easily translates that energy in her photos.

Last but not least, a heartfelt thanks goes to my amazing friends and family, including my loving husband, John, and my two sons, Jack and Walt, who are always immensely supportive of my thirst for knowledge and my wild pursuits.

FOREWORD

As the chief planner and historic preservation officer for the City of Dallas, I am constantly asked, "What is historic in Dallas?" While such a question can seem both maddening and ignorant, I cannot help but understand and sympathize with the reasoning behind such a statement. Like many Sun Belt boomtowns, Dallas is blessed with a booming economy and a short-term memory of history or of its humble beginnings.

While Fort Worth, its sister city, has been dubbed "Where the West Begins," Dallas has sometimes been given the unfortunate tag of "Where the East Peters Out." Though it is considered an insult by some, there is some truth to the label. Dallas's history is not readily apparent at first glance and is far more complex and rich than many realize. Dallas is indeed where the East "petered out," but also where the Republic of Texas pushed northward from the Gulf Coast, where remnants of the Old South ended, where cotton was once king and where cutting-edge technologies were developed and revolutionized. Dallas is educated and cultured enough to once have supported the largest bookstore in the world, but it was, at one time, a hub of Ku Klux Klan activity. To this day, struggles with institutional racism cripple large swaths of the city. Dallas bore the horrific assassination of a president on its streets, earning it the shameful nickname "City of Hate," only to reemerge in the ensuing decades as the birthplace of "America's Team" and the stomping ground of television's lovable villain J.R. Ewing.

Dallas is home to more than 150 (and counting) individual landmarks, parks, cemeteries and neighborhoods that are deemed official city landmarks. Overall, these designations encompass more than four thousand structures that are representative of all types and styles of late-nineteenth- and twentieth-century architecture. Gracing neighborhoods, commercial districts, parklands and public spaces, these sites are illustrative of how, with modern urban planning theories, the historic is able to meld with—and indeed enhance—the modern cityscape.

And yet, despite the erasure of iconic buildings and humble neighborhoods from the local landscape and lexicon, there remains a steady and strong undercurrent of memories and remembrances for natives and a deep desire for newcomers who have chosen to make Dallas a place to bloom and thrive. As people search for places to settle that are authentic and have a story, the collection, preservation and honoring of such sites and the narratives that accompany them become even more important.

With *A History Lover's Guide to Dallas*, Georgette Driscoll has done a masterful job of delving deep into the many levels of Dallas's often painful but always colorful past to allow the reader to take a complex and complete journey to truly understand the city's heart and soul—the good and the bad. Please enjoy and take the time to peel back the many layers of the great city of Dallas.

—Mark Doty

1

BIRTH OF THE BIG D

(PRE-1839–1870)

There is little evidence of a prolonged Native American presence where modern-day Dallas is located. The rarity of artifacts has left the impression that the area was not used as a permanent encampment but more for hunting expeditions and travel to other Caddo communities. It is believed that Dallas was not a permanent settlement until the early 1800s, when the first white settlers arrived.

In 1839, John Neely Bryan, a frontiersman, left Arkansas in search of the ideal location to start a training post in North Texas. He was attracted to the upper banks of Trinity River, as the Republic of Texas already had plans to create a nearby road, the Preston Trail, which would serve as the main transportation route between central and north Texas. He staked his claim near the Three Forks of the Trinity River with sticks and some stones, then returned to Arkansas to settle his affairs. He made it back to Texas in 1841 to find that most of his potential customers were gone, as a treaty had forced most of the local Native Americans to leave northern Texas.

Bryan decided to create a permanent settlement and persuaded several families from nearby Bird's Fort (close to modern-day Irving) to join him. In 1843, he married the daughter of one of these families, Margaret Beeman, and they had five children. They settled near the east bank of the Trinity River, where it narrowed to create a natural crossing location. Bryan operated a ferry to cross the Trinity where Commerce Street crosses the river today. A reconstruction of Bryan's original 1841 log cabin can be seen in Founders Plaza, located downtown on Main Street.

The *Cattle Drive* sculptures commemorate the nineteenth-century longhorn cattle drives along the Shawnee Trail. The sculptures, including forty-nine life-size steer and three trail riders, were created by Robert Summers and are located at Pioneer Plaza adjacent to Pioneer Park Cemetery. *Photograph by the author.*

Bryan then began trying to convince others to move to his town. There are stories stating that he gave lots of land to newly married couples and may have held a lotto for land rights. The start of the town was a hard sell, as the roads were primitive, and the Trinity River and creek crossings were problematic. Even with these challenges, by 1844, the townsite of Dallas had been surveyed, and the land was laid out in half-mile square blocks and streets. The origin of the name Dallas is unknown but can be found in records dating back to 1842. Some believe it was named after Commodore Alexander Dallas, a well-known naval hero. Another theory is it was named after vice president of the United States George Mifflin Dallas.

During the same period, the Republic of Texas was actively promoting settlement in the north central region. One promotion included providing approximately ten million acres of land to Williams S. Peters, an English businessman who had immigrated to the United States in 1827. Together with his associates and investors, he established the Peters Colony. To attract farming families, they granted 640 acres of free land to those who would build their homes in the area. The Peters Colony was widely advertised and attracted many settlers. Due to the land grant, these settlers were able to spend their cash on other resources and needs, such as hiring teachers.

One of the most successful Peters Colony settlements was north of modern-day Dallas. Although it was originally called Mustang, the settlers changed the name to Famers Branch due to the rich soil and abundance of crops. The Keenan, Webb and Gilbert families were instrumental in the growth of the area, and it soon became one of the best-known and most attractive settlement areas in Texas. Isaac Webb donated land for the Webb's Chapel Methodist Church, which also served as the first school. Dr. Samuel Gilbert and his wife, Julia, built a stately dogtrot-style home, which can still be seen at the Farmers Branch Historical Park. Farmers Branch Cemetery (Keenan Cemetery) is thought to be the oldest cemetery in Dallas County. Established in 1843, it is located near the Rose Gardens and the Farmers Branch City Hall on Webb Chapel Road in Farmers Branch.

Texas was admitted into the United States of America as the twenty-eighth state on December 29, 1845. Dallas County was formed in 1846, with Dallas serving as the temporary county seat. Texas's entry into the Union further encouraged immigration from nearby states and abroad. The 1850s census included 163 people in the town (2,743 in Dallas County), including two Germans and a dozen people from England and Ireland. Dallas quickly grew as a service town for the settlements and rural areas surrounding it, and voters selected Dallas as the permanent county seat in 1850. At the time, the town included a general store, drugstore, saloon, insurance agency, brickyards and a weekly newspaper, the *Dallas Herald*. On February 2, 1856, Dallas was granted a town charter, and Dr. Samuel Pryor was elected the first mayor.

After purchasing what remained of John Neely Bryan's property in Dallas, Alexander and Sarah Cockrell moved from their 640-acre Peters Colony land grant to Dallas and quickly became major business leaders. Their enterprises included a sawmill, lumberyard and a freighting business. They also erected a lucrative toll bridge that crossed the Trinity River and opened access into Dallas. In 1858, Alexander Cockrell was shot and killed by the town marshal, Andrew M. Moore, who was in debt to Cockrell. Alexander's widow, Sarah, continued to operate and expand their businesses, including a luxury hotel, the St. Nicholas. She regularly bought, sold and leased land. When she died in 1892, she was one of the richest people in Dallas and owned approximately one quarter of modern-day downtown Dallas, over 2,500 acres in Dallas County and additional properties throughout the state.

In addition to the influence from the original town settlers and those from the Peters Colony, La Reunion greatly impacted the future of Dallas. La Reunion was a utopian community formed in 1854 by French, Belgian and Swiss colonists. La Reunion's population quickly grew to 350 people and contained highly educated professionals, scientists, artists, musicians and naturalists. However, the La Reunion colonists lacked the agricultural knowledge needed for survival in the foreign land. The land they purchased was primarily limestone and hard to farm, resulting in massive food shortages. By 1857, the colony, which had been located near the three forks on the Trinity River, had disbanded, and many of the skilled settlers moved to Dallas. Those who remained on the La Reunion land were also brought into the city folds as their land was incorporated into Dallas in 1860.

By 1860, the town population had grown to 678, including 97 African Americans, most of whom were enslaved. Abraham Lincoln won the 1860 presidential election, and the following year, Dallas County voted 741–237 in favor of secession. Texas left the Union in early 1861 and joined the Confederate States of America. Most of the citizens of Dallas were very supportive of the Confederacy, and many men enlisted. Many parades were held, and citizens gave money and supplies to the Confederate army. Dallas was far from any battles and suffered no direct damage from the Civil War.

On June 19, 1865 (Juneteenth), Texas slaves were liberated. Many former Texas slaves moved to Dallas, as it was more prosperous than other parts of the state. Agents from the Bureau of Refugees, Freedmen and Abandoned Lands (a.k.a. Freedmen's Bureau) who were assigned to Dallas faced a hostile climate, with many locals refusing to follow the legislation and courts refusing to enforce them. Freedmen's towns were scattered throughout the city and on the periphery of Dallas. The Tenth Street Historic District, on the eastern edge of Oak Cliff, is one of the oldest relatively intact freedmen's towns in Dallas. A freedmen's town in North Dallas that was later known as State-Thomas grew to at least 500 citizens. Deep Ellum, just north of downtown, was also established as a freedmen's town and eventually became a mecca for jazz and blues artists.

Many white southerners also moved to Dallas during Reconstruction. The thriving city, with both business and agricultural options, attracted many transplants from towns that were rebuilding after the Civil

War. The Ku Klux Klan first appeared in Dallas in 1868. Poor local organization, federal legislation and state measures helped reduce the Klan's presence in Texas. Although the Klan started to wane, its existence was still observable in Dallas, and racial oppression greatly impacted the residents and the culture of the town that was experiencing vast growth and transformation.

YOUR GUIDE TO HISTORY

Freedman's Cemetery was established in 1861 as a burial ground for Dallas's early African American population and is one of the largest freedman cemeteries in the county. The memorial was built in 1990. *Photograph by the author.*

Dallas Heritage Village at Old City Park
Downtown
1515 South Harwood Street
214.413.3679
www.dallasheritagevillage.org
Admission charge

Dallas Heritage Village is home to the largest collection of nineteenth-century pioneer and Victorian homes and commercial buildings in Texas. There are also more than twenty-four thousand objects, including tools and implements, furnishings, domestic accessories, photographs and postcards that represent the period from 1840 to 1910.

Dallas Heritage Village is located on the thirteen acres where Dallas's first park, City Park, and zoo were located. In 1967, the Dallas County Heritage Society moved the Millermore, an antebellum mansion, into the park. The Millermore Mansion, completed in 1857, was home to William Brown Miller, one of Dallas County's early settlers. Miller owned a ferry service that operated on the Trinity River, and he grew cotton on his 7,500 acres. Although Miller was incredibly successful, his Greek revival mansion was crumbling by the 1950s. Concerned citizens saved the mansion from demolition by moving it to the park, where it has since been restored. It became the first of many other nineteenth-century and Victorian historic buildings that were saved from demolition by being moved to the park.

The City of Dallas still owns the park and buildings, but the village is operated by the Dallas County Heritage Society. The society has collaborated with the Dallas Jewish Historical Society, the Dallas Mexican American Historical League and Remembering Black Dallas to ensure the village represents the diverse historic neighborhoods of Dallas in the early 1900s.

Visitors may take a self-paced tour of the museum and grounds. Guided and group tours are also available. If visiting with little ones, be sure to linger at the Learning Lounge, which provides a great interactive play space. There are no restaurants on site, but snacks and drinks are available at the ticket office. Picnic lunches are welcome and recommended. Dallas Heritage Village provides a variety of programs for all ages. Some programs are seasonal, while others offer opportunities for learning throughout the year. Check the website for current classes and events.

Farmers Branch Cemetery (Keenan Cemetery)
North/Farmers Branch
12501 Webb Chapel Road, Farmers Branch
Free

Farmers Branch Cemetery is thought to be Dallas County's oldest cemetery. It is located near the Rose Gardens and Farmers Branch City Hall on Webb Chapel Road. Established in 1843, it was originally named Keenan Cemetery. Thomas and Sarah Keenan came to the area as part of the Peters Colony. Their two-month-old son, John, passed away in 1843 and is buried at the cemetery. The number of infant graves speaks to the hardships faced by early pioneers. Thomas and Sarah Keenan and many of their descendants are also buried here. The town of Farmers Branch occasionally offers living history cemetery tours.

Founders Plaza
Downtown/Corner of Market and Elm Streets
Free

Founders Plaza is located in the heart of downtown Dallas. The recently renovated open park includes the Old Red Courthouse, a re-creation of the 1840s log cabin John Neely Bryan built near the Trinity River, the Philip Johnson–designed Kennedy Memorial and a fountain with seating areas.

Freedman's Cemetery and Memorial
Uptown/Corner of Lemmon Avenue and North Central Expressway
Free

Located next to the Greenwood and Jewish Cemeteries just off the North Central Expressway is the Freedman's Memorial Cemetery. The small cemetery was established in 1861 and serves as the resting ground for more than five thousand former slaves, with many unmarked graves. The last recorded burial occurred in 1925. In the 1990s, a memorial was built to commemorate the contributions of African Americans to the growth of Dallas. Powerful sculptures by renowned artist David Newton are included in the impressive entrance and centerpiece.

The original 1840s cabin built along the Trinity River by John Neely Bryan, the founder of Dallas, was lost in a flood. This re-creation, built in the 1930s, can be found downtown in Founders Plaza. *Photograph by the author.*

HARWOOD STREET HISTORIC DISTRICT

Downtown/East Side, including portions of Harwood, Elm, Main, Commerce, Jackson, Wood, Young and Canton Streets

Free

Harwood Street Historic District is a commercial district located on the east side of downtown. It served as a major commercial area and connected residential areas to downtown. The district includes significant structures like the Majestic Theatre, Hart Furniture Building, Dallas Hilton, Masonic Temple and First Presbyterian Church. The buildings in the district were constructed from the 1880s through the 1950s, with architectural styles that include Italianate, Beaux-Arts, neoclassical revival, Renaissance revival and art deco. Many of the buildings have been renovated and repurposed to be mixed-use. The Majestic Theatre still serves as a performance hall and is also home to the administrative offices for the City of Dallas Office of Cultural Affairs. The area became a Dallas Landmark District in 1990.

Heritage Farmstead Museum
Far North/Plano
1900 West Fifteenth Street (Normal F. Whitsitt Parkway/TX-FM544), Plano
972.881.0140
www.heritagefarmstead.org
Admission charge

The Heritage Farmstead Museum is located on the land of the 1891 farmhouse built by Hunter Farrell, a successful businessman. The farm was managed by Mary Alice Farrell and her daughter Ammie until 1972, when Ammie passed away. After a seven-year, $1.2 million restoration project, the Heritage Farmstead Museum opened to the public.

The four-and-a-half-acre historic farm complex has been awarded designation by the Plano Landmark Association, a State of Texas Historical marker and a listing in the National Register of Historic Places. The Heritage Farmstead Association has also received accreditation from the prestigious American Association of Museums. The Heritage Farmstead Museum contains over ten thousand objects and archival materials. These objects relate to Blackland Prairie life in North Texas from the 1890s to 1920. The vast collection is used to furnish the museum's historic buildings.

Self-guided tours include the grounds and allow visitors to view animals and the outside of the buildings. Self-guided tours do not include access to the Farrell-Wilson House, Young House or School House. However, a printed guide is provided. Docent-guided tours are available. Reservations are required for guided tours for parties of six or more. Family days, camps and other learning programs are available throughout the year.

Peak's Suburban Addition Historic District
Northeast of downtown and Deep Ellum; bounded by Fitzhugh,
Sycamore, Peak, Haskell and Worth Streets
www.peaksaddition.org
Free

Peak's Suburban Addition began when Colonel Jefferson Peak built a large estate at the corner of Worth and Peak Streets in 1855, one year before Dallas was granted a town charter. Colonel Peak's home was the first brick home, and the neighborhood that followed is the oldest residential neighborhood in modern-day Dallas. After the Civil War, more wealthy families, including the Gastons, moved to the area to build large country estates and stately Victorian homes. However, due to an economic downturn, building slowed until the turn of the century.

Starting in 1903, promotion and development were renewed in the area. Some of the large country estates were divided, and an abundance of Prairie and Craftsman homes were built. As the economy recovered, Dallas started to expand, and Peak's Suburban Addition Historic District started to experience commercial encroachment along streetcar lines and at major intersections.

By the 1920s, the neighborhood had shifted from being a suburban neighborhood with single-family homes to a highly populated urban hub on the eastern outskirts of a bustling downtown. Around the same time, apartments became popular dwelling spaces for the burgeoning population, and apartment complexes, such as the 1924 Viola Court Apartments at 4845 Swiss Avenue, started to appear along streetcar lines.

The Peak's Suburban Addition Historic District, which spans twenty-two city blocks and includes 350 buildings, is unique in that the architectural styles span several decades. The eclectic collection includes residential, church and apartment buildings in Queen Anne, Prairie, Mission revival, Tudor, art deco and classical architectural styles. The proximity of Peak's Suburban Addition to downtown and the steady development of the neighborhood display a wide range of Dallas's developmental and architectural history.

PIONEER PLAZA AND PIONEER PARK CEMETERY
Downtown/Dallas Convention Center District
1428 Young Street
Free

Located in the convention district of downtown Dallas near Young and South Griffin Streets, Pioneer Plaza is a four-acre public park with a stream and small waterfall. It is one of the most visited destinations in Dallas due to the 1993 addition of the Texas Longhorn *Cattle Drive* sculpture. Created by artist Robert Summers of Glen Rose, Texas, it is the largest outdoor bronze sculpture in the world. It includes forty-nine bronze steers and three trail riders and commemorates the nineteenth-century cattle drives that traveled along the Shawnee Trail.

Adjacent to the park is Pioneer Park Cemetery, which contains the remnants of four separate cemeteries—the Masonic Cemetery, Odd Fellow's Cemetery, Jewish Cemetery and City Cemetery. Burials took place from the 1850s to 1921. It includes the remains of several members of the city's earliest families. Although John Neely Bryan is buried in Austin, Texas, the cemetery also contains a memorial to him.

St. Paul United Methodist Church
Downtown
1816 Routh Street
214.922.0000
www.stpaulumcdallas.com
Free

Located in the Dallas Arts District on Routh Street across from Booker T. Washington High School, St. Paul Methodist Episcopal Church was established in 1873 by recently freed slaves. The congregation originally met in a brush arbor. In 1901, Dallas's first black architect (and Booker T. Washington's son-in-law), Sidney Pitman, started to design the brick building that still stands today. It took twenty-six years to build, with congregants fundraising and collecting bricks for the structure one by one. At its height, the congregation had over 1,600 members and was the cornerstone of the freedmen's town. As Dallas expanded and the surrounding freedmen's town was razed, the congregation diminished, but the church remained downtown despite the gentrification of the area. The building was designated as a historic landmark by the City of Dallas, is a Texas Historical Landmark and is listed in the National Register of Historic Places. In 2009, the building underwent major renovations and the church still operates today.

State-Thomas
Uptown, bounded by Woodall Rogers Freeway, Bryan Place and U.S. Route 75
Free

State-Thomas has a long and diverse history. The area just north of Dallas was originally a freedmen's town that was created immediately after emancipation. At the close of Reconstruction, the area was incorporated into the city of Dallas in 1874, and some of the area became a neighborhood for the elite. As early as 1875, mule-drawn streetcars were providing wealthy residents with transportation to downtown. Some early residents included George Bannerman Dealey, publisher of the *Dallas*

Cattle Drive sculptures at Pioneer Plaza. *Courtesy of Donna Kidby.*

The founder of Dallas, John Neely Bryan, passed away in Austin, Texas, where he had been admitted to the Texas State Lunatic Asylum. This memorial marker in Pioneer Park Cemetery was erected in 1954 in Bryan's honor. *Photograph by the author.*

Morning News, and Herbert M. Greene, partner at the Green, LaRoche and Dahl architectural firm.

As Dallas grew, much of the original freedmen's town was razed and paved over during the construction of the Central Expressway. The remaining six blocks are a Dallas Landmark District in the Uptown area. State-Thomas contains a diverse blend of architectural styles, including shotgun style and Prairie-influenced homes. However, State-Thomas is best known for having the largest collection of Victorian homes remaining in Dallas, with roughly 60 percent of the Victorian homes in State-Thomas built prior to 1899. The Jacob and Eliza Spoke House, located at 2600 State Street, is listed in the National Register of Historic Places and is a grand example of Victorian homes of the era.

Tenth Street Historic District
Oak Cliff, bounded by East Clarendon Street, South Fleming Street, Interstate 35 East, East Eighth Street, East Ninth Street and Plum Street
Free

Tenth Street Historic District is one of the oldest freedmen's towns in Dallas and one of the only remaining intact freedmen's towns in the nation. A starter neighborhood for black emigrants soon after the Civil War, the district still contains many of the original buildings constructed between 1890 and 1940. Buildings consist of various styles in folk designs. The Greater El Bethel Baptist Church, on Ninth Street, dates to 1886. Modest residential buildings date to as early as 1910 and are relatively unchanged, illustrating the great skill and craft of the builders. In 1994, the Tenth Street Historic District was listed in the National Register of Historic Places in recognition of the area's architectural value and cultural significance.

2

BOOMTOWN

(1871–1901)

By 1870, Dallas was the largest town in North Texas, with a population of around three thousand. The citizens took great pride in how much growth had occurred over thirty years. The city that had started with the goal of being a trading post had become a bustling county seat and lively trading center. The town was also home to many skilled workers serving the residents of surrounding areas for their legal matters, insurance and medical needs. Dallas was quickly becoming a boomtown.

Centrally located in North Texas, Dallas was in a prime location for trade, and although the site of the town was selected, in part, due to its proximity to the Trinity River, the river came with complications. The Trinity River, which runs 715 miles, is the longest self-contained river in Texas. Projects that attempted to make it navigable failed, as this would have required extensive dredging. The citizens of Dallas remained landlocked. In addition to contributing to the isolation citizens felt, the Trinity River also brought devastation, as major flooding was a persistent threat.

Another body of water, Browder Springs, also had a significant impact on Dallas becoming a boomtown. Located a mile southeast of the Dallas County Courthouse, Browder Springs served two major roles in Dallas's history. A private company purchased two acres and the spring from Lucy Jane Browder and turned these into the first municipal water supply, initially producing three hundred thousand gallons of water per day.

The second impact from Browder Springs came during the securing of a Texas & Pacific (T&P) rail line for Dallas. The T&P was planning to route the line roughly fifty miles north of Dallas, but in a deceptive effort to ensure Dallas received the benefit of the line, Representative John W. Lane of Dallas attached a rider to legislation requiring that the line must cross within a mile of Browder Springs. The bill passed without the state legislature realizing that Browder Springs was a mile from the Dallas County Courthouse. T&P officials were furious, but Dallas voters approved a cash grant, bonds and land for a train depot to ease the pain that resulted from this legislative trick.

The T&P line was actually the second rail line for Dallas, making the city the first rail crossroads in the state and a major hub for shipping and distribution. Dallas residents had previously voted to approve a land and money grant to lure the Houston & Texas Central (H&TC) to Dallas. A historical marker for the original intersection of the T&P and H&TC railways in 1873 can be seen on Pacific Avenue under Interstate 45. You can book a train trip on an 1896 locomotive through the Grapevine Vintage Railroad or learn more about the railroad industry at the Museum of the American Railroad.

Telegraph lines, which tended to come with railroads, and a new bridge crossing the Trinity River further linked Dallas to the world and nearby towns. Business boomed, and Dallas became the headquarters for many merchants. The population soared, including an emergence of a large professional sector, and land values skyrocketed. By 1880, the Missouri-Kansas-Texas (MKT or Katy) Railroad also reached Dallas, and the population grew to 10,385. By 1890, Dallas was the most populous city in Texas, with 38,067 residents. East Dallas and Oak Cliff were annexed in 1890 and 1904, respectively, resulting in another population boom and a large geographic expansion.

Residents of the Dallas area included migrants from Texas and other southern and northern states. Foreign immigrants also came to Dallas to seek jobs and opportunity. German, Italian and Hispanic settlers worked on rail crews and established businesses, including newspapers, restaurants and markets, that catered to the needs of their communities. The African American population grew to 21 percent of the city's 1890 population despite the discrimination and political disfranchisement they faced.

Similar to other frontier boomtowns, Dallas also experienced an influx of gunfighters, train-robbers and con men. One notorious resident was John Henry Holliday, a.k.a. "Doc" Holliday, who had moved west seeking a drier climate to ease his tuberculosis symptoms. In 1874, he opened a dentist's office in Dallas on Elm Street between Market and Austin Streets.

The Old Red Courthouse was built downtown in 1892. Four of the previous five courthouses had perished in fires, and as such, county officials were determined to build a courthouse that would last. The courthouse now serves as the Old Red Museum of Dallas County History and Culture. *Photograph by the author.*

As his tuberculosis cough worsened, he lost patients and started to rely on gambling for his income. While in Dallas, he was arrested for illegal gambling and trading gunfire, and he left the state after being tried and found guilty of "gaming." In the years to come, Holliday gained a fierce reputation as a gambler and ruthless gunman. After befriending Wyatt Earp and fighting alongside him at the O.K. Corral, he would become one of the most recognizable figures of the Wild West.

In 1877, Benjamin Long, a La Reunion colonist who became a two-term mayor of Dallas, was shot and killed in a saloon after confronting a man who refused to pay his bar bill. This, and similar Wild West incidents, spurred local merchants and more community-driven settlers to subdue the more nefarious side of the city. In addition to focusing on enhanced law enforcement and city services, citizens also started to focus on leisure, culture and education opportunities.

Today, the City of Dallas maintains over four hundred parks. The land for the city's first park, City Park, which is now home to Dallas Heritage Village, was purchased in 1876. The land was naturally beautiful and included Browder Springs. It was enhanced with the addition of paved walkways, flowerbeds and, later, a bandstand. City Park also became home to the first zoological garden in the state when two mountain lions and two deer were purchased in 1888. The zoo was briefly moved to Fair Park before moving to its permanent home in Marsalis Park in Oak Cliff in 1912.

Women played a major role in the cultural and environmental development and success of the city. The city's upper- and middle-

The Trinity River and its many tributaries often flooded. Improvements have reduced the chances of flooding today, but the early floods were often disastrous to the burgeoning city. This picture captures a train attempting to cross at Turtle Creek in May 1908. *Courtesy of Dallas Municipal Archives.*

class women formed multiple social and literary clubs that focused on raising funds for worthy causes, political involvement and volunteer work. May Dickson Exall united several of the clubs and organized the Dallas Federation of Women's Clubs in 1898. The group's first campaign involved raising funds and support for a free public library in Dallas. After the city received a $50,000 grant from Andrew Carnegie, the first Dallas Public Library was built in 1901 on the corner of Commerce and Harwood Streets in downtown. Additional achievements by women's organizations included the creation of the Dallas Arts Association, the introduction of health and child care options and many other city beautification projects.

Successful businessmen and manufacturers developed elegant new neighborhoods on the outskirts of the bustling city. Stately Victorian homes were built on the south side of downtown in a neighborhood called the Cedars. The Cedars became home to lawyers, politicians and a thriving Jewish community. As industry and business continued to expand, the wealthy moved on, seeking to distance themselves from the city. Unfortunately, little remains of the original Cedars homes, as most of them were demolished to make way for highway expansion in the 1960s.

Highland Park is well known for its multimillion-dollar homes and famous residents. The main road, Lakeside Drive, runs parallel with Turtle Creek and is buffered by over fourteen acres of immaculately landscaped green space. *Courtesy of Donna Kidby.*

Other neighborhoods, such as the exclusive Highland Park neighborhood along Turtle Creek, survived the city's growth. Highland Park was designed at the turn of the century by George Kessler, who planned Fair Park, and landscape designer Wilbur David Cook, who planned Beverly Hills, California. Roughly 20 percent of the original land was set aside for parks within the neighborhood. Although the city of Dallas made multiple attempts to annex Highland Park, it remains a separate town. It continues to be the most affluent area in Dallas (and the fourth-most affluent area in Texas) and is home to the Dallas Country Club.

Munger Place was the first deed-restricted neighborhood in Texas, and Swiss Avenue was the first paved street in Dallas. Prominent Dallas families hired nationally renowned architects to build quality homes in Renaissance, Tudor, Craftsman and Georgian revival styles. Swiss Avenue was designated as Dallas's first historic district, and home tours showcasing the diverse architectural styles popular in the early twentieth century are available throughout the year. Just east of Munger Place, Junius Heights was created in 1906. It is Dallas's largest historic district, consisting of more than eight hundred Craftsman and Prairie homes.

Woodrow Wilson High School, located in the Lakewood neighborhood, opened in 1928 and still operates as a school. *Photograph by the author.*

If you tour the old east Dallas neighborhoods, be sure to make a stop at the Lakewood Theater, built in 1938. The art deco building and one-hundred-foot iconic neon sign are well-known landmarks in East Dallas. Nearby, Woodrow Wilson High School, designed by Dallas architect Mark Lemmon, is also a treasure. The Elizabethan style building opened in 1928 and served as the only East Dallas high school until 1957. The school still operates as part of the Dallas Independent School District.

These neighborhoods were created by people who wanted to escape the congestion and dangers associated with downtown. Downtown buildings were unregulated and erected too quickly to accommodate the speedy growth. Most had short life spans, as fires easily spread throughout the packed city. By 1890, Dallas had already had five courthouses, four of which had perished by fire. After a fire in 1890, the city started to build its sixth courthouse at the corner of Main and Houston Streets on land donated by John Neely Bryan and his wife, Margaret. "Old Red" was finished in 1892 and served as the county courthouse until 1966. The building was added to the National Register of Historic Places in 1976 and now serves as the Old Red Museum of Dallas County History and Culture.

Although Dallas was hit hard by financial panic toward the end of the century, it swiftly recovered. The restored growth helped ignite workers. The American Federation of Labor granted a charter to the Trades Assembly of Dallas in 1899. One of the earliest victories included the eight-hour workday. Locals George Clifton Edwards, Dean Stuck and George Hindsdale joined together and successfully pushed child-labor laws through the Texas legislature in 1903. Even with laws preventing child labor, limited opportunities and economic deprivation contributed to children being pushed into work in the factories and mills.

Taxation for schools was defeated in multiple local proposals, and a formal public school district was not established until 1884. The first schools were in rented structures with little to no money for books or supplies. When the first public school district, the Dallas Independent School District, was formed, six schools were already operating—four schools for white children and two segregated schools for African Americans. Colored School No. 2 was established in 1892 as a high school for African Americans and moved to a larger building in 1922 and renamed Booker T. Washington High School. For many years, it was the only Dallas high school that allowed African Americans to enroll. The building, located at 2501 Flora Street, now serves as a performing and visual arts public magnet school located in the Dallas Arts District.

Booker T. Washington High School, located in the Dallas Arts District, was built in 1922. For many years, it was the only high school in Dallas that allowed African Americans to attend. The school is still in operation and now serves as a performing and visual arts public magnet school. *Courtesy of Donna Kidby.*

Education expansion in the city also included colleges, with Southern Methodist University (SMU) opening in 1911. The first SMU building, Dallas Hall, was designed by Shepley, Rutan and Coolidge and remains the university's centerpiece. The building opened its doors in 1915 and is listed in the National Register of Historic Places. Additional historic colleges have since moved to Dallas, including Paul Quinn College (founded in 1872 in Austin) and Dallas Baptist University (founded in 1898 in Decatur).

The foundation laid by early settlers helped attract skilled workers, farmers and business owners to Dallas. Migration brought more diversity to the town. The railroad expansion created greater trade opportunities, and Dallas quickly turned into an industrialized city as early timber constructions were replaced with lavish steel and ornate stone buildings. Major institutions helped streamline and protect urban life; this effort included the creation of municipal departments to address health, safety, education and public works. Original geographic limitations were expanded due to annexations and the wealthy building elite neighborhoods on the outskirts of the city. The geography of the town further expanded with the introduction of freemen's towns, neighborhoods created by and catering to immigrants and the development of "streetcar suburbs" due to new mass-transit systems. By 1900, Dallas was not just a boomtown but the third-largest city in Texas.

YOUR GUIDE TO HISTORY

Dealey Plaza was built for the 1936 Texas centennial in downtown Dallas and named in honor of George Bannerman Dealey, longtime publisher of the *Dallas Morning News*. Dealey Plaza instantly became world-famous in 1963 after the assassination of President John F. Kennedy. *Courtesy of Donna Kidby.*

Booker T. Washington High School
Downtown
2501 Flora Street

This, the first school for African Americans in Dallas, was established in 1892. In 1922, the school moved to Flora Street. For many years, it was the only high school in Dallas that allowed students of color. Under court order, the school was desegregated in 1976 and was redistricted as a magnet school for students who are artistically gifted. The surrounding neighborhood has evolved into the Dallas Arts District, and the school still serves as an arts magnet school in the Dallas Independent School District. The original 1922 portion of the campus is still intact and is a historical landmark.

Cathedral Santuario de Guadalupe
Downtown
2215 Ross Avenue
214.871.1362
www.cathedralguadalupe.org
Free

The first Catholic parish in Dallas, Sacred Heart Church, was established in 1869. The original church was built at the corner of Bryan and Ervay Streets. In 1890, Sacred Heart was designated as the diocesan cathedral and soon outgrew its church building. Land was purchased at the corner of Ross and Pearl Streets, and the cornerstone for Cathedral Santuario de Guadalupe was laid in 1898. The cathedral was formally dedicated in 1902. Today, the cathedral serves the largest cathedral congregation in the United States, serving 630,000 Roman Catholics in the nine-county Diocese of Dallas. It also has the largest Latino parish congregation in the United States, and services are presented in both English and Spanish.

Located in the Dallas Arts District, Cathedral Santuario de Guadalupe is the largest cathedral congregation in the United States, serving 630,000 Roman Catholics. *Courtesy of Donna Kidby.*

Dallas Farmers Market
Downtown
1010 South Pearl Expressway
214.664.9110
www.dallasfarmersmarket.org
Free

South Pearl has been a hub for wholesale farm sales since the late nineteenth century. By 1941, the site was officially sanctioned as a municipally owned and operated market. The thriving market offers a great variety of food with seasonal variations. Vendor and produce listings are available online. Check the market's official hours of operation before you plan your trip.

Dallas Firefighter's Museum
East/Fair Park
3801 Parry Avenue
214.821.1500
www.dallasfiremuseum.com
Admission charge

The Dallas Firefighter's Museum provides fire safety education, honors fallen heroes and helps preserve firefighting history. Vintage tools, memorabilia and historic photos are on display. The "Dallas Pike," a firefighting tool used to rip through tongue-and-groove ceilings, was invented by members of the Dallas Fire Department. The highlight of the museum is "Old Tige," a horse-drawn water pump that was used in Dallas from 1884 to 1911.

The museum is located across from the main entrance from Fair Park and was an active station from 1907 to 1975. This station had the first horse hospital for the Dallas Fire Department. A sick horse would be taken to this station to receive treatment and would be returned to its station when it was once again fit for duty.

In the 1960s, the Dallas Fire Council approved the formation of a museum and chose the Fair Park station for this purpose. The building was designated as a City of Dallas landmark and opened as a museum in 1972.

The Dallas Firefighter's Museum, located near Fair Park, is home to "Old Tige," a horse-drawn water pump that was used in Dallas from 1884 to 1911. *Courtesy of Donna Kidby.*

Dallas Zoo

South of Downtown
650 South R.L. Thornton Freeway
469.554.7500
www.dallaszoo.com
Admission charge

The Dallas Zoo dates from 1888, when the City of Dallas purchased two deer and two mountain lions from a man in Colorado City for sixty dollars. Originally located in City Park (currently Dallas Heritage Village), it was the first zoological garden in the state.

The zoo was then briefly located in Fair Park but moved to its permanent home in Marsalis Park in Oak Cliff in 1912. Numerous fundraising campaigns were held, and by 1920, the zoo had over one thousand animals. In 1925, schoolchildren in Dallas raised the funds to purchase Queenie the elephant, who lived at the zoo through 1955.

Through numerous community campaigns, support from the City of Dallas and help from the federal Works Progress Administration (WPA), the zoo continued to grow and was named one of the ten largest zoos in the country by 1940. In the 1950s, the Dallas Zoological Society was founded with the sole purpose of raising funds to purchase new animals for the collection.

Through the remainder of the 1900s, the zoo continued to expand, adding more focus on research and conservation. In the early 2000s, the zoo had some rough years, including a gorilla escape in 2004. By 2009, the City of Dallas had turned over management of the zoo to a private organization, and by 2010, the completion of the Giants of the Savanna exhibit brought new community confidence.

Indeed, there should be confidence in the Dallas Zoo, as it has earned numerous accolades, including being listed in the "Nation's Top 10 Zoos" by *USA Today* and as having the best African zoo exhibit, according to *Zoobook*. Today, the Dallas Zoo features a 106-acre park, thousands of animals and an education department that offers programs for all ages.

A sixty-seven-foot-tall giraffe (and the tallest statue in Texas) greets visitors at the entrance, preparing them for the unique experience they will have when visiting the Giants of the Savanna exhibit. Unlike at many zoos, where visitors see giraffes at a distance, one is eye to eye with these charming animals in Dallas. The Dallas Zoo has been recognized as being the first zoo in North America to combine giraffes, elephants, zebras, impalas, ostriches and more together in the Giants of the Savanna habitat.

Another major attraction is the Wilds of Africa exhibit, an eleven-acre African savanna that includes every major habitat of the continent. The Monorail Safari takes guests on a one-mile tour through six habitats, and many of the animals in this exhibit can only be viewed from the monorail.

The massive zoo includes many other exhibits, including cheetah encounters, a hippo outpost, a lemur lookout and much more. The Lacerte Family Children's Zoo includes ponies for riding and birds to feed. If you get hungry, head to the Serengeti Grill, which has floor-to-ceiling observation windows and often features a lion lazing right against the glass.

DEALEY PLAZA
Downtown
500 Main Street
Free

Dealey Plaza was built for the 1936 Texas Centennial in downtown Dallas and named in honor of George Bannerman Dealey. Dealey was president and general manager of the *Dallas Morning News*. He was instrumental in the growth and planning of Dallas near the start of the twentieth century. He helped bring the Federal Reserve Bank to Dallas and assisted with the establishment of Southern Methodist University. He participated in many civic boards, including the Commission on Interracial Cooperation, and he was extremely vocal and influential in the opposition to the Ku Klux Klan.

Dealey Plaza became instantly world-famous in November 1963, when it became the site of the assassination of President John F. Kennedy. The Sixth Floor Museum is located across Elm Street, and the John F. Kennedy Memorial is a little farther east on Main Street.

DEEP ELLUM

East, roughly bounded by Interstate 75, Interstate 30, Elm Street and First Avenue
www.deepellumtexas.com
Free

Deep Ellum started in the late 1800s as an African American residential and commercial neighborhood. Settled as a freedmen's town by former slaves, it is located on Elm Street east of the Houston & Texas Central tracks. At the time, the area was considered to be too far from downtown to be desirable. In addition to the African American community, the area also included many manufacturing plants, including the Continental Gin Company and the Ford plant.

Starting in the 1920s, the area was a hotbed for blues and early jazz. Blind Lemmon Jefferson, Lead Belly, Blind Willie Johnson, Mance Lipscomb, Alex Moore and T-Bone Walker all spent their early years playing in Deep Ellum. It became well-known as one of the major entertainment districts for African Americans not just in Dallas but across the South. Today, Deep Ellum still has plenty of local music venues and is considered one of the musical centers in Texas.

Designed by William Sidney Pittman, the Knights of Pythias Temple was built in 1916. Located at 2551 Elm Street, the temple was the first major commercial structure built by African Americans in the city. The multipurpose building included storefronts for retail shops and offices for professionals and served as a cultural center with the state headquarters of the Grand Lodge of the Knights of Pythias. The city designated the site as a Dallas Landmark in 1989.

The Sons of Hermann is a national fraternal organization that promoted German culture and heritage. The organization started a Dallas chapter in the 1890s and moved its headquarters to Elm Street in 1910. The headquarters served as a dance hall and meeting place. The building is the oldest freestanding wooden structure in Dallas and still serves as an event and music hall.

Visit Deep Ellum to see the city's largest collection of preserved storefronts from the early twentieth century; these now house locally owned shops, music venues, restaurants and galleries. Many of the early manufacturing plants, including that of the Continental Gin Company, are still intact and have been restored and repurposed as multi-use complexes that contain space for lofts, restaurants and retail shops. As you enter the area, you will be welcomed by the thirty-eight-foot-tall *Traveling Man* sculpture. There is also a community-wide mural project and plenty of public art on view.

J. Erik Jonsson Central Library
Downtown
1515 Young Street
214.670.1400
www.Dallaslibrary2.org
Free

In 1898, the Dallas Federation of Women's Clubs was founded by May Dickson Exall. The group's first campaign involved raising funds and support for a free public library in Dallas. A $50,000 grant from Andrew Carnegie led to the construction of the first Dallas Public Library in 1901 on the corner of Commerce and Harwood Streets. The building was torn down and replaced by a contemporary six-story facility in 1954. Although this building still stands, it too became overcrowded, and in 1984, the central facility was moved to a new building at the corner of Young and Ervay Streets, across from city hall.

Even if you live or are staying in another part of town, be sure to plan a trip to one of the largest public library facilities in the nation. The J. Erik Jonsson Central Library, named in honor of the mayor who played a major role in its development, has eight floors full of treasures, including Shakespeare's *First Folio* (1623) and one of the original broadside copies of the Declaration of Independence (printed on July 4, 1776).

Grapevine Vintage Railroad
Grapevine Station: 705 South Main Street, Grapevine
Fort Worth Stockyards Station: 130 East Exchange Avenue, Fort Worth
817.410.8136
grapevinetexasusa.com/grapevine-vintage-railroad.com
Admission charge

The Grapevine Vintage Railroad operates two engines. "Puffy" is a 1896 Cooke locomotive originally used in California for passenger and freight service. "Vinny" is a 1953 Diesel 2199 that was originally operated by the Santa Fe Railroad. These two engines pull four 1925 day coaches and two 1927 open-air touring coaches that have been fully restored to their Victorian-era glory.

Grapevine Vintage Railroad offers a variety of seasonal and special train experiences throughout the year. One of the most popular is the Cotton Belt

Route, a ninety-minute ride from Main Street in Grapevine to the historic Fort Worth Stockyards. Shorter excursions, including the Trinity River One-Hour, are available. Special event rides are available throughout the year, like the Trick or Treat and North Pole Express.

The trains run ten months out of each year, with no service in January or February. The schedule includes rides on Saturdays and Sundays. Friday options are also available in the summer months. Prices vary based on train ride and seating. Limited food and drink options are available for purchase.

Junius Heights Historic District
East of Munger Place, south of Swiss Avenue and southwest of Lakewood
Free

Junius Heights is Dallas's largest historic district, consisting of more than eight hundred homes. Located in East Dallas and just south of the Swiss Avenue historic neighborhood, the district was established as a streetcar development, and the main building period was between 1900 and 1940. The dominant style is Craftsman bungalow, but there are also many Victorian cottages and Prairie homes. The eclectic district also includes some Tudors, colonial, neoclassical and other styles of houses.

McKinney Avenue Trolley (M-Line)
Uptown
214.855.0006
www.mata.org
Free

The original transportation system in Dallas was powered by mule-drawn cars in the 1870s. Electric cars were in place by 1888, with a line traveling from Peak to Elm Streets and through downtown and along Jefferson Street to Cockrell Hill Road. By the 1930s, more than three hundred streetcars were in operation in the area.

By the middle of the twentieth century, there was a push to provide more parking, make more room for cars and "modernize the city." Dallas abandoned its last streetcars in 1956. Demand for the nostalgic ride brought trolleys back to Dallas in July 1989.

The McKinney Avenue Transit Authority runs the M-Line, which normally runs 365 days a year on a 2.8-mile track through the charming shopping and dining Uptown district. The fully restored, air-conditioned and heated vintage trolleys are free to ride and operate throughout Dallas's Uptown neighborhood.

Much like during the 1930s, when downtown had more than three hundred streetcars in operation, the M-Line trolley offers free rides through uptown, downtown and the Dallas Arts District. *Photograph by the author.*

Museum of the American Railroad
North/Frisco
6455 Page Street, Frisco
214.428.0101
www.museumoftheamericanrailroad.org
Admission charge

The Museum of the American Railroad opened in 1963 at Fair Park. As the years passed, it became apparent that the museum needed more space and the opportunity to keep the collection away from the elements. In 2008, the museum found its new home in Frisco, Texas, about thirty miles north of downtown Dallas. The museum's collection includes a wide variety of artifacts and archival material from the railroad industry and cars and locomotives from the early twentieth century.

Old Red Museum of Dallas County History and Culture
Downtown
100 South Houston Street
214.745.1100
www.oldred.org
Admission charge

The land at the corner of Main and South Houston Streets was donated to the county in 1850 by John Neely Bryan, founder of Dallas, and his wife, Margaret. "Old Red" was built on the land in 1892. Old Red gets its name from the Pecos red sandstone that was used to build the large courthouse. When the Romanesque building was complete, it became the county's sixth courthouse on this land. Four of the previous five had perished by fire, and as such, county officials were determined to build a courthouse that would last.

Old Red did last and served as the county courthouse until 1966, then was repurposed as the State Department of Public Welfare. After some remodeling for various uses and a degree of neglect, local historians voiced a need to preserve the historic courthouse. It was added to the National Register of Historic Places in 1976, and restoration began soon after.

Today, Old Red is home to the Old Red Museum of Dallas County History and Culture. The restoration included bringing back many authentic features and architectural delights, including the ninety-foot-tall clock tower. The entire building serves as a testament to the craftsmanship of the time, including the fully restored Hatton W. Summers courtroom on the fourth floor.

The museum's exhibits include a focus on Dallas's early years, the city's transformation into a trading center, the "Big D" developments and current culture. The museum shop, drinks and snacks, docent tours and facility rentals are available.

SOUTHERN METHODIST UNIVERSITY (SMU)
Park Cities
Dallas Hall: 3225 University Boulevard
www.smu.edu
Free

Southern Methodist University (SMU) was chartered in 1911 by the southern denomination of the Methodist Episcopal Church. The first building at the university, Dallas Hall, is now listed in the National Register of Historic Places. Dallas Hall was designed by Shepley, Rutan and Coolidge and remains the university's centerpiece. The building opened its doors in 1915 to 456 students and 37 faculty members.

SMU's main campus is still located in the Highland Park and University Park areas. As of 2013, SMU became the home of the George W. Bush Presidential Center and Library on twenty-three acres on the southeast side of campus. SMU is a very selective university with high academic standards and is consistently recognized as one of the top universities in the United States.

SWISS AVENUE AND MUNGER PLACE HISTORIC DISTRICTS
Swiss Avenue: Northeast of Downtown/Along Swiss Avenue
between La Vista Drive and Fitzhugh Avenue
Munger Place: Between North Fitzhugh, Gaston, Henderson and Columbia Avenues
www.sahd.org
www.mungerplace.com
Free

In 1905, Robert S. Munger and his brother Collett built the "City Man's Home" just minutes from downtown Dallas. Swiss Avenue, a wide boulevard named by Swiss immigrant Henri Boll, became the first paved street in Dallas. Prominent Dallas families hired nationally renowned architects to build quality homes in Renaissance, Tudor and Georgian revival styles. The neighborhood was the first deed-restricted neighborhood in Dallas, and over two hundred elegant homes were built by 1920.

After years of neglect from the Great Depression through the 1960s, restoration began on the homes in the 1970s. Interested citizens and the Historic Preservation League (now known as Preservation Dallas) made great efforts to preserve the neighborhood. The result was a huge success. The Swiss Avenue Historic District became the city's first historic district in 1973 and includes the largest collection of Prairie-style homes in America. The neighborhood is a wonderful place to stroll, and home tours are periodically offered.

TEXAS FIRE MUSEUM
West Dallas
2600 Chalk Hill Road
214.267.1867
www.texasfiremuseum.org
Free

The Texas Fire Museum occupies the former Dallas Fire Department Maintenance Facility in West Dallas. The facility was restored by volunteers and includes exhibit halls, a library and a restoration shop. In the restoration shop, hand-drawn, horse-drawn and motorized fire apparatus are restored by skilled mechanics and artisans. Call before making an outing to the Texas Fire Museum, as the hours are limited and can vary.

WEST END HISTORIC DISTRICT
Downtown
Includes the west side of Ross Avenue, Elm Street, Main Street and Jackson Street
www.dallaswestend.org
Free

The first trading post was opened by John Neely Bryan in what is now known as the West End Historic District. In the late 1800s, the area dramatically grew due to the railroad presence. Now, visitors to the West End can enjoy museums, a variety of restaurants, clubs and shopping.

Wilson Block Historic District
North of Deep Ellum
Wilson House: 2922 Swiss Avenue
Free

The Meadows Foundation owns and operates the Wilson Block Historic District, which includes twenty-two acres of turn-of-the-century Victorian and Queen Anne buildings. It contains the largest collection of late-nineteenth-century houses in Dallas.

Fredrick and Henrietta Wilson acquired the land from Henrietta's uncle, who had come to Texas as part of the La Reunion colony. The Wilsons built their home, an elegant 1899 Queen Anne Victorian mansion, in the area. The Wilsons also built six additional homes as rental properties. As the city grew, commercial buildings started to encroach on the neighborhood. Real estate developers looked to raze many of the homes to make way for new buildings.

The Wilson Block was preserved through the efforts of the Historic Preservation League, which had enlisted the help of the Meadows Foundation. The Meadows Foundation restored the Wilson Block homes and moved other houses that were endangered to the area. The houses have been repurposed as office spaces and are provided rent-free to thirty-nine nonprofit agencies. Preservation Dallas, which offers research and preservation services, now occupies the Wilson House. The district is recognized as a City of Dallas Landmark District and is listed in the National Register of Historic Places.

3

WILDCATS AND WILD EXPANSION

(1901–1950)

On October 31, 1930, seventy-year-old Columbus Marion "Dad" Joiner was hiding from angry mobs in a Dallas hotel. Three years earlier, Dad, a former lawyer and Tennessee legislator, headed to Texas with forty-five dollars in his pocket. In Dallas, he became a sweet-talking wildcatter and promoter. He soon set out to northeast Texas and easily acquired leases on several thousands of acres of land from poor farmers in Rusk County. He started to sell one-acre interest certificates using fabricated reports provided by his friend and self-taught geologist A.D. "Doc" Lloyd. By reselling certificates to multiple investors, Joiner was able to raise enough money to purchase a rig and start drilling.

Geologists from the major oil companies said there was no possibility of oil in Rusk County, but Dad trusted Doc and moved forward with his prospecting. The first two wells were dry and crippled the old and rusty equipment. Not deterred, Joiner continued to oversell his certificates to finance the operation. On September 3, 1930, a drill stem test at the third well produced a surge of oil. H.L. Hunt, an Arkansas and Oklahoma oilman who had been invited to the event, quickly leased the surrounding tracts of land. Within two weeks, the Joiner's well gushed oil in front of over five thousand spectators, many of whom were celebrating what they thought to be their newfound fortune. However, the investors swiftly learned they had been swindled, and the courts took action. Creditors began searching high and low for Dad Joiner.

Dallas's Fair Park was the site for the 1936 Texas Centennial Exposition. In addition to the financial benefit of hosting the exposition, Dallas benefited due to the great improvements made at Fair Park, including the addition of more than fifty art deco buildings and multiple sculptures. The *Tenor* statue is located at the Esplanade. *Courtesy of Donna Kidby.*

H.L. Hunt had suspicions that the oil ran farther than anyone imagined. Hunt found Joiner at the Baker Hotel in downtown Dallas and convinced him to sell 5,580 acres for $1.3 million—more money than Joiner had ever imagined and enough to settle the claims against him.

Hunt's purchase is known as the "Black Giant," an oil reservoir forty-three miles long and twelve and a half miles wide. Since 1930, more than thirty thousand wells have been drilled, which have yielded more than five billion barrels of oil. The Black Giant is still producing today. Hunt Oil Company incorporated in 1934 and moved to Dallas in 1937. By 1948, Hunt was labeled the richest man in the nation by *Fortune* magazine. Today, Hunt Oil Company is one of the largest privately held companies in the United States and still operates domestically and internationally.

The Texas oil boom, "the gusher age," actually started almost thirty years before the Black Giant was discovered. The first major strike was at Spindletop, close to Houston, in 1901. This strike gained national attention and spurred Texas oil exploration, including the wildcatting undertaken by Dad and Doc, and brought rapid changes to Texas. Oil discoveries also brought investors, prospectors, laborers and businessmen to Dallas.

At the turn of the century, Dallas had one of the world's largest cotton markets, and the Dallas Cotton Exchange was organized in 1907. Dallas also became one of the top manufacturers of cotton-ginning machinery. Agriculture and ranching, the chief economic drivers, were quickly replaced by industrialization, with Dallas becoming home to many refineries and processing plants. The opening of the Federal Reserve Bank in 1914 and a Ford assembly plant also greatly impacted the growth of the city. Many of the early manufacturing plants, including the Continental Gin Company in Deep Ellum, are still intact and have been restored and repurposed as multi-use complexes.

Not all the wealth in Dallas was due to oil and manufacturing. A growing city required large retail, hospitality and construction industries. In 1907, Herbert Marcus, Carrie Marcus Neiman and Al Neiman opened a luxury retail store. Within weeks of opening (and in spite of the Panic of 1907), Neiman Marcus was instantly successful and quickly sold through all of its lavish clothing stock. Neiman Marcus stores brought a new level of cosmopolitan culture to Dallas and became a pioneer in the American retail experience. The headquarters of Neiman Marcus are still located in downtown Dallas on Main Street near South Ervay Street. It's also very fitting that Highland Park Village Shopping Center, developed in 1931, has the distinction of being the first planned shopping center in the United States.

The same year Neiman Marcus opened, the 1907 Praetorian Building was completed and was among the first skyscrapers in Texas. In 1912, the Adolphus Hotel was constructed on Commerce Street and served as the first grand hotel in the city. The Adolphus Hotel welcomed many big bands, stars and even presidents and queens over the years. Listed in the National Register of Historic Places, the Adolphus still serves as a luxury hotel.

Until the twenty-nine-story Renaissance Revival Magnolia Petroleum Building opened in 1922, the Adolphus was the tallest building in Texas. The building served as the headquarters for Magnolia Petroleum Company and is now also a luxury hotel. In 1934, a forty-two-foot-wide and forty-foot-tall red Pegasus, the symbol for Mobil Oil, was added to the top of the building to welcome attendees to that year's petroleum convention. The Pegasus—which rotated and was lit at night, when it could be seen for miles—quickly became a Dallas landmark and icon that was said to be watching over Dallas. The Pegasus was taken down in 1999 due to structural issues and was replaced in 2000. The original Pegasus has been restored and can be seen on top of a twenty-two-foot oil derrick in front of the Omni Hotel on Lamar Street.

Big D's growth also came in the form of military presence. Love Field has origins as an army camp used to train prospective pilots during World War I. Love Field was named in honor of First Lieutenant Moss L. Love of the Eleventh Calvary. He lost his life in a crash in 1913 and was the tenth fatality in U.S. Army aviation. After the war, the camp at Love Field was deactivated as an active duty airfield, and the city of Dallas purchased the land in 1927, opening the airfield for civilian use. In 1929, Delta started the first passenger service at Love Field.

Fair Park was also briefly used as an army training facility called Camp Dick from 1918 to 1919. Fair Park is a Dallas Landmark and was

Love Field had its origins as an army camp where prospective pilots trained during World War I. The Love Field Band is pictured here in 1918. *Courtesy of Dallas Municipal Archives.*

added to the National Register of Historic Places in 1986. What is now a 277-acre park that is used annually as fairgrounds started with the 1886 Dallas State Fair and Exposition. Since then, a fair has been held every year at Fair Park (with a few exceptions during World War I and World War II, including when it served as Camp Dick). The State Fair of Texas is currently recognized as one of the most highly attended fairs in the United States and is the signature event in Dallas each fall. Big Tex, a fifty-five-foot-tall cowboy statue wearing size seventy boots and a seventy-five-gallon hat, has been a recognizable symbol for the fair since its introduction in 1952.

The location for the Dallas State Fair and Exposition was selected due to its proximity to the eastern outskirts of downtown and the low price for the land. By 1890, the fair attracted nearly thirty-five thousand visitors. A fire in 1904 created great financial loss for the owners, who sold the land to the City of Dallas but kept the rights to hold an annual fair. After purchasing the property, the city took the opportunity to transition the land into Dallas's second public park and rightfully named it Fair Park. George

Capped by a bald eagle, the Tower Building at Fair Park is a stunning structure that was built in 1936 for the Texas Centennial Exposition. *Courtesy of Donna Kidby.*

Kessler, landscape architect and city planner, played a major role in the development of the park by encouraging the City Beautiful Movement. The City Beautiful Movement advocated for tree-lined walkways, fountains, public art and natural beauty.

One of the major milestones for Fair Park and Dallas came when Fair Park was selected for the Texas Centennial Exposition of 1936, the state's official observance of the Texas revolution centennial. Robert L. Thornton, a banker who later became known as "Mr. Dallas," was instrumental in securing Dallas as the location for the celebration. During the exposition, visitors came to Dallas from every state and many countries throughout the world. With more than six million visitors in six months, the exposition not only helped Dallas weather the Depression-era economy, it also put Dallas in the news as a sophisticated, urban city.

The benefits of the exposition also included the construction of more than fifty buildings. Local architect George Dahl was selected to design the buildings. The result was masterful and is one of the most significant art deco sites in the United States. Today, the buildings are used for the African American Museum, Children's Aquarium, Texas Discovery Gardens, South Dallas Cultural Center and other attractions. The Dallas Historical Society, which was formed in 1922, is located in the Hall of State, which was designed and built as the centerpiece of the exposition, with the *Tejas Warrior* focusing attention on the building's grand entrance. Another well-known building, the Cotton Bowl, has hosted many collegiate rivalries since the 1930s and was the first home of the Dallas Cowboys.

Unfortunately, there is a long history of racial discrimination associated with the park and the State Fair of Texas. By the 1920s, the Ku Klux Klan had been reborn, and Dallas is thought to have had the largest chapter in the world. Plenty of Klan candidates were voted into political power. The State Fair of Texas was segregated, with only a few days designated for African Americans to attend, and in 1923, the State Fair designated a Ku Klux Klan day.

When the Texas Centennial Exposition arrived in 1936, federal assistance was needed to fulfill the commitment to creating an African American exhibit, the Hall of Negro Life. Although it was built, Centennial officials obscured the building, and it was the only building demolished after the exposition. Today, the African American Museum of Dallas sits on the same land where the Hall of Negro Life was originally built for the exposition.

The Hall of State building at Fair Park now houses the Dallas Historical Society, which formed in 1922. The *Tejas Warrior* statue focuses attention toward the building's grand entrance. *Photograph by the author.*

Maceo Smith, publisher of the *Dallas Express* and deputy director of the Hall of Negro Life at the exposition, fought against school segregation and served on the national board of directors at the National Association for the Advancement of Colored People (NAACP). Under his leadership, the NAACP greatly expanded in Texas and became the second-largest chapter in the nation. Smith joined with Maynard Jackson Sr. (father of Maynard Jackson Jr., who became the first African American mayor of Atlanta) to form the Progressive Voters League in 1936.

Great strides were made against the Klan with support from the NAACP and local activists and supporters, most notably the *Dallas Morning News* and George Bannerman Dealey, president of the *News*. In addition, a newly formed Dallas County Citizens League denounced the Klan as an un-American organization and demanded that public officials who belonged to it resign.

The Klan countered with a reign of terror, arousing fear and hatred of African Americans, Jews, Catholics, Hispanics and foreigners in general. Many Klan members were in powerful positions in the business and public sectors. The white elite continued to dominate the political power and reserved most of the city funds and services for white business owners and residential districts.

Dirt road in Dallas, circa 1928. *Courtesy of Dallas Municipal Archives.*

One neighborhood that was severely underserved was "Little Mexico," a neighborhood that started when a large number of Mexican immigrants arrived in Dallas seeking refuge and work during and after the Mexican Revolution (1910–20). The conditions were very poor, homes were overcrowded and disease soon became rampant. The area—bounded by Maple Avenue, McKinney Avenue and the Missouri-Kansas-Texas Railroad—has since been redeveloped as Uptown, with few remaining signs of the former neighborhood. Pike Park, established in 1913 and located on Harry Hines Boulevard, is one of the few intact structures from the community.

National attention to the abuse coming from Klan members and internal disagreements regarding the opposition to Jews and Catholics slowly started to turn the tide of Klan power. In 1924, the Klan was unsuccessful in gaining the governorship in Texas. Miriam "Ma" Ferguson defeated the pro-Klan candidate and became the first female governor of Texas. In 1925, David Stephenson, a national Klan leader, was convicted of second-degree murder and sentenced to life in prison. The realization that the Klan was losing political power, along with public disgraces, helped reduce Dallas Klan membership from 13,000 (in 1924) to 1,200 (in 1926). Nevertheless, the Klan had influenced the racial beliefs of many Dallas citizens, and these prejudices created great impact for decades.

Construction of expressways in the 1940s cut through the freedmen's towns, and many African American communities were disbanded. As African Americans moved to other areas of the city, they were accosted with bombings. As national attention was given to the bombings, the politicians and businessmen of Dallas realized that the racist atmosphere would be a detriment to the image of Dallas, a city that was once again seeing another period of large industrial growth during and after World War II. The bombings ceased after an investigation led to thirteen indictments, but there were no convictions.

By 1950, Dallas's population had reached almost 435,000 and was highly segregated. Although the 1954 Supreme Court ruled that segregation in public schools was unconstitutional, the Dallas School Board delayed integration for nearly a decade. With support from civil rights activists like Juanita J. Craft, protests were staged at segregated lunch counters, restaurants and theaters. Most of the downtown stores desegregated by 1962, and many schools and theaters followed the next year. Although civic leaders were forced into integration, for the most part, Dallas's politics remained ultraconservative and for the white elite. The urban image favorable to businesses remained intact, and the city attracted many new businesses focused on aircraft manufacturing, auto assembly, wholesale trade and technology.

YOUR GUIDE TO HISTORY

The Adolphus Hotel opened in 1912, serving as a luxury hotel in downtown. The hotel, which still operates today, has welcomed many special guests, including presidents and queens. *Photograph by the author.*

Adolphus Hotel
Downtown
1321 Commerce Street
214.742.8200
www.adolphus.com

Adolphus Busch, founder of the Anheuser-Busch Company, set out to create the city's first grand hotel. The result was the Adolphus, a twenty-two-story Beaux-Arts style building that opened in October 1912. The site of the Adolphus, at the corner of Commerce and Akard Streets, was the site of the city hall building from 1889 to 1910. When Busch bought the land, city hall was razed to make room for the hotel.

Until the neighboring Magnolia Petroleum Building opened in 1922, the Adolphus Hotel was the tallest building in Texas. In the 1920s, the hotel opened the Century Room on the nineteenth floor. It was a welcome home for many of the big bands and stars of the era, including Tony Bennett, Benny Goodman and the Andrew Sisters. Over the years, the Adolphus also broadcasted live radio with special appearances by Bob Hope and Kate Smith. Special guests have included Queen Elizabeth II and Presidents Jimmy Carter and George H.W. Bush. Listed in the National Register of Historic Places, the Adolphus still serves as a Dallas landmark and a luxury hotel.

Bishop Arts District
Southwest of Downtown, bounded by North Tyler Street, West Ninth Street,
North Zang Boulevard and West Davis Street
www.bishopartsdistrict.com
Free

Bishop Arts District is located southwest of downtown Dallas and just east of Winnetka Heights, Dallas's second-largest historic district full of Prairie-style homes. The area was originally developed in the 1920s, providing shops for nearby residents. By the 1930s, a trolley stop on Davis Road had become Dallas's busiest stop. Due to retail and neighborhood shifts in the 1960s, the area started to decline. In 1984, local developers Jim Lake Sr. and Mike Morgan purchased many of the storefronts and set out to preserve and revitalize the area.

Today, Bishop Arts District includes a wide variety of independent galleries, boutiques, antique stores and restaurants to suit any taste. The area is very trendy but also provides a small-town feel just outside of downtown. Many events and festivals are held in the district, including Wine Walks and the Oak Cliff Film Festival.

BONNIE AND CLYDE

Bonnie Parker's gravesite
Northwest
Crown Hill Cemetery
9718 Webb Chapel Road

Clyde Barrow's gravesite
West
Western Heights Cemetery
1613–99 Fort Worth Avenue

In the 1920s and 1930s, West Dallas consisted of industrial buildings and modest, poverty-stricken housing. This unincorporated part of Dallas was known as the "Devil's Backdoor." With little resources and few options, criminal behavior was the norm, and it was here that one of the most notorious couples in American history met.

Bonnie Parker was born in Rowena, Texas, in 1910. Her family moved to West Dallas after the death of her father when she was four years old. Clyde Barrow came by way of West Dallas when his poor farming family moved from Ellis County. The couple met in 1930 and were immediately smitten with each other.

Their two-year, Depression-era crime spree ran from 1932 to 1934. With their gang, Bonnie and Clyde set out across the Midwest, robbing banks, rural stores and gas stations. They gunned down several police officers and some civilians who tried to stop them.

On May 23, 1934, Texas Rangers tracked down the couple and ambushed them in Louisiana. Over 130 rounds were fired into their car on a rural road, and Bonnie and Clyde are said to have been shot more than 50 times each. Services for each of them were held in Dallas, and both were buried in West Dallas. Clyde is buried in Western Heights Cemetery. Bonnie was originally buried at Fishtrap Cemetery, but her remains were moved in 1945 to Crown Hill Cemetery, where her mother and brother are also buried.

The inscription on Bonnie's marker reads: "As the flowers are all made sweeter by the sunshine and the dew, so this old world is made brighter by the lives of folks like you."

The remains of Bonnie and Clyde were returned to Dallas after their crime spree ended with them being killed. Bonnie Parker's grave is located in Crown Hill Cemetery. *Photograph by the author.*

THE CHILDREN'S AQUARIUM AT FAIR PARK
East/Fair Park
1462 First Avenue
469.554.7340
www.childrensaquariumfairpark.com
Admission charge

Northeast of Leonhardt Lagoon at Fair Park, the Hall of Aquatic Life was built in time for the 1936 Texas Centennial Exposition. The aquarium, the first in Texas and the twelfth built in the United States, was a huge success and wildly popular. It featured forty-four tanks that hosted a variety of fish, reptiles and amphibians. In 1938, the name was changed to the Dallas Aquarium. The original director, Pierre A. Fontaine, was in place until his passing in 1968. During his tenure, he kept close watch over the aquarium and ensured its success.

After Fontaine's passing, the aquarium suffered from severe neglect and lost its accreditation. Fortunately, bonds were provided for a complete renovation. In 2010, it opened to the public restored and with a new name—The Children's Aquarium.

The redesign is perfect for little ones, with many of the exhibits at the right eye level for the pre-K set. There are opportunities to touch and feed fish and many interactive exhibits. A weekly fish-feeding demonstration schedule is posted on the aquarium's website.

Although it was one of the largest aquariums in the country when it was built, it is considered a small venue by today's standards. This is actually a bonus for a children's aquarium, as it can all be seen without overextending a young child's energy or interest level. There are six exhibit areas, including freshwater, intertidal, shore, near shore and offshore habitats. Outside is Stingray Bay, which includes a large tank with cownose rays, southern stingrays and sharks.

Annual passes are available, and Dallas Zoo memberships provide discounted admission rates.

DALLAS HOLOCAUST MUSEUM CENTER FOR EDUCATION AND TOLERANCE

Downtown/Historic West End District
211 North Record Street, Suite 100
214.741.7500
www.dallasholocaustmuseum.org
Admission charge

The Dallas Holocaust Museum Center for Education and Tolerance is located in Dallas's Historic West End. It is one of a few Holocaust-related museums in the United States and the only Holocaust museum serving Texas, Oklahoma, Arkansas and Louisiana. It was founded in 1984 and is dedicated to teaching the history of the Holocaust and advancing human rights.

The museum includes a core exhibit, museum archives and library and special exhibits that often include guests and speakers, such as Holocaust survivors. The Core Exhibit focuses on one day during the Holocaust: April 19, 1943. On this day, three important events occurred: The Twentieth Deportation Train from Mechelen, Belgium, was attacked by resistance fighters; the Warsaw Ghetto Uprising began; and the Bermuda Conference met. The exhibit dedicated to these three different events, which are artfully woven together, illustrates heroism, resistance and appreciation for the strength and perseverance needed for humans to overcome brutality and hatred.

Fair Park
East/Fair Park
Interstate 30 East: Exit 47, Second Avenue and Fair Park
Interstate 30 West: Exit 47C, First Avenue and Fair Park
From Downtown: East on Commerce, right on Second Avenue

Friends of Fair Park
214.426.3400
www.fairpark.org
Free

The east Dallas site of the current Fair Park was selected by a group of Dallas businessmen planning a fair and exposition. The 1886 Dallas State Fair and Exposition included exhibit facilities and a racetrack on eighty acres of land. Although attendance was estimated at more than 100,000 guests, fair revenues fell short of costs. Although the fair was popular and well attended, financial troubles continued to grow each year due to repeated fires and the 1903 ban on horse-race gambling.

In 1904, the owners sold the fairground property to the City of Dallas but retained rights to hold an annual fair and exhibition. The city took the opportunity to transition the land into Dallas's second public park and named it Fair Park. In 1905, the fair association was reorganized as the State Fair of Texas name, and that year, Fair Park hosted more than 300,000 guests. By 1916, attendance grew to one million.

Fair Park continued to develop and the State Fair of Texas continued to grow during the 1920s. However, one of the major milestones came when Fair Park was selected for the Texas Centennial Exposition of 1936. More than $25 million was earmarked for construction. Local architect George Dahl was selected to reconstruct the buildings. The result was an art deco masterpiece. As one of most significant art deco sites and one of the largest assemblages of exposition buildings in the United States, Fair Park was added to the National Register of Historic Places in 1986 and became a Dallas Landmark in 1987.

The Women's Museum Building welcomes visitors to Fair Park. The building is one of many art deco structures that were created for the 1936 Texas Centennial Exposition. *Courtesy of Donna Kidby.*

Over the years, the park grounds have expanded to include 277 acres and thirty structures. The annual State Fair of Texas is still held there every fall and is recognized as one of the most highly attended fairs in America. In addition to the fair, numerous sports, cultural and entertainment attractions are held year-round in the beautifully restored art deco buildings and on the vast grounds. Amongst other great attractions, the African American Museum, Children's Aquarium, Hall of State and Texas Discovery Gardens are all located at Fair Park.

LAKE CLIFF HISTORIC DISTRICT
Southeast of Downtown, just east of Interstate 35 East

Lake Cliff Historic District includes Lake Cliff Park, which, in 1906, served as an amusement park and contained a giant pool, waterslides, a skating rink and theaters. The amusement park surrounded a large man-made lake that dates back to 1888 and was originally known as Spring Lake but was later renamed Lake Cliff. The amusement park was wildly popular but proved to be too expensive to operate. The land was sold to the city in 1914.

The city redesigned the park with a more naturalistic focus. Today, the park is still a beloved green space and serves as the central focus of the historic district, with baseball fields, playgrounds, gardens and picnic areas surrounding the sunken freshwater lake.

The residential section of the historic district dates to the 1920s and 1930s and includes one- and two-story Prairie, Craftsman and Tudor revival homes as well as multiple apartment buildings. The thirteen-story Lake Cliff Tower Hotel was built in 1929 at 329 East Colorado Boulevard and still dominates the skyline.

MAGNOLIA HOTEL
Downtown
1401 Commerce Street
214.915.6500
www.magnoliahotels.com/dallas-downtown.com

When the twenty-nine-story Magnolia Building was completed in 1922, it became the tallest building in Dallas and one of the tallest buildings in the country. The building was erected as the headquarters for the Magnolia

The Pegasus is a Dallas icon that has watched over the city since it was added to the roof of the Magnolia Building in 1934. A reconstruction still lights the night sky from atop the Magnolia. The original Pegasus is now located in front of the Omni Hotel downtown. *Photograph by the author.*

Petroleum Company, which developed from the gains of the Spindletop strike and was a precursor to the Mobil Oil Company. The Magnolia Building is now a luxury hotel and was added to the National Register of Historic Places in 1978.

The building is easily recognizable with the iconic glowing red Pegasus on top. The red Pegasus, the symbol for Mobil Oil, was added in 1934 to welcome attendees to that year's petroleum convention. The forty-two-foot-wide and forty-foot-tall red Pegasus rotated and was lit at night. Easily visible for miles, it quickly became a Dallas landmark and icon. In the 1970s, the Pegasus stopped rotating, and it was taken down in 1999 due to structural issues. The current owners of the Magnolia Building had a re-creation made, and at midnight on New Year's Eve in 2000, the Pegasus once again started to serve as a Dallas beacon. The original Pegasus has been restored and can be seen on top of a twenty-two-foot oil derrick in front of the Omni Hotel on Lamar Street.

NEIMAN MARCUS BUILDING
Downtown
1618 Main Street
Flagship Store: 214.741.6911
The Zodiac restaurant: 214.573.5800

In 1907, Herbert Marcus, Carrie Marcus Neiman and Al Neiman opened a luxury retail and specialty store. Within weeks of opening, Neiman Marcus was instantly successful and quickly sold through all of its lavish clothing stock. Neiman Marcus brought a new level of cosmopolitan culture to Dallas.

After a fire burned the previous store on Elm Street, Neiman Marcus opened a new store at the corner of Main and Ervay Streets in 1914. The Renaissance revival building is listed in the National Register of Historic Places and serves as an important reminder of Dallas's retail history. Today, the building serves as the corporate headquarters and flagship store for the Neiman Marcus chain, which has become internationally recognized as a fashion innovator and pioneer of the modern retail experience. The Zodiac, located on the sixth floor, is an elegant lunch restaurant that has been serving the elite of Dallas for over fifty years.

SOUTH BOULEVARD AND PARK ROW HISTORIC DISTRICT
Southeast of downtown, bounded by Park Row Avenue, South Boulevard
and Edgewood Street and Atlanta Street
www.southblvdparkrow.org
Free

As the city expanded at the turn of the century, the desire for cleaner and quieter neighborhoods drove development away from the downtown center. One such expansion was the movement of many of Dallas's successful entrepreneurs south of Old City Park to South Boulevard and Park Row. When Temple Emanuel El relocated to South Boulevard in 1913, many of the city's prominent Jewish families followed. The majority of the residents of South Boulevard and Park Row were wealthy Jewish merchants, including the Khan, Linz and Marcus families. Herbert Marcus, cofounder of Neiman Marcus, and his family lived at 2620 South Boulevard.

Many of the Prairie, Mission and Craftsman style homes were designed by prominent architects of the time, including Lang & Witchell, George Dahl and Roscoe DeWitt. The exuberance of the 1920s shows in the flamboyant motifs. The district has a common architectural bond with the Swiss Avenue Historic District, which was built farther east during the same time period and was designed by many of the same firms.

In the 1950s, the synagogues moved to North Dallas, and South Boulevard no longer held status as a prominent Jewish community. Continued city growth and the highway expansion in the 1960s also impacted the neighborhood. However, nine blocks consisting of over one hundred intact and stunning homes built between 1910 and 1935 remain and make for an excellent walking tour of the district.

Texas Discovery Gardens in Fair Park
East/Fair Park
3601 Martin Luther King Jr. Boulevard
214.428.7476, ext. 341
www.texasdiscoverygardens.org
Admission charge

The Hall of Horticulture was built in Fair Park for the Texas Centennial Exposition in 1936. The building included the first public conservatory in the Southwest, and after the exposition, the building transitioned into the Dallas Garden Center. In addition to serving as a garden center, it was also the headquarters of war rationing during World War II and the women's building during the State Fair of Texas from 1945 to 1949.

Over time, new gardens and changes to the building were added, and it was renamed Texas Discovery Gardens in 2000. With a new name came a new mission, which includes "teaching effective ways to restore, conserve, and preserve nature in the urban environment."

Today, Texas Discovery Gardens includes seven and a half acres, and all of the gardens are certified as 100 percent organic. There are ten themed gardens, including a butterfly habitat, native wildlife point, scent garden, share garden and an heirloom garden. All the collections feature native plants with a select few species from other regions. All plants are selected based on the habitat benefits they provide for native wildlife, including butterflies, bugs and birds.

The interior is filled with natural wonders, as well. Although there have been additions to the original building, much of the work on the facility has been to restore it to its original 1936 appearance, complete with bas-relief panels depicting native North Texas plants and insects.

One fantastic addition was the Rosine Smith Sammons Butterfly House and Insectarium. Inside the two-story structure, visitors can enjoy immersion in a tropical rainforest, complete with hundreds of free-flying butterflies, more than sixty species of tropical plants and rotating insect and arthropod displays. Be sure to visit at noon, when the daily release of newly emerged butterflies is held in the Butterfly House.

Texas Discovery Gardens hosts guided tours, gardening workshops, plant sales and events and festivals throughout the year. A wide variety of educational classes are available for both adults and children.

WHEATLEY PLACE HISTORIC DISTRICT

South Dallas, bounded by Warren Avenue, McDermott Avenue,
Meadow Street and Malcolm X Boulevard
Free

Wheatley Place Historic District is named after Phillis Wheatley, an African American poet from the eighteenth century. The neighborhood was a suburban development specifically built for black families from 1916 to 1940. The district was home to many influential black citizens, including G.B. Garner and John B. Rice, both members of the Negro Chamber of Commerce. Among the early twentieth century bungalows is the home of civil rights pioneer Juanita Craft. The district was added to the National Register of Historic Places in 1995 and designated a Historic Landmark District in 2000.

WINNETKA HEIGHTS

Southwest of downtown, roughly bounded by Davis Street, Rosemont Avenue,
Twelfth Street and Willomet Avenue
www.winnetkaheights.org
Free

Winnetka Heights was originally part of Oak Cliff but was replatted in 1908, when prominent businessmen set out to develop the fifty-square-block area and turned it into a prestigious neighborhood. Several members of the Dallas elite, including L.A. Stemmons, built large Prairie-style homes in the desirable neighborhood that provided easy access to Dallas's central business district. Most of the homes were completed by 1922, and the neighborhood has maintained its character and charm.

In 1981, Winnetka Heights became the sixth historic district adopted by the City of Dallas. With over six hundred residential structures and twenty commercial structures, it is the second largest historic district in Dallas. The homes reflect the architectural styles of the early 1900s, with wonderful examples of Prairie, Bungalow and various other eclectic styles. The home of J.P. Blake, one of the developers, still stands at 401 North Rosemont Street and is home to the Oak Cliff Society for Fine Arts. The commercial component is mainly along West Davis Street, where the structures date from the early development of the neighborhood.

The Winnetka Heights Neighborhood Association has taken on many projects, including protecting and preserving the mature landscape and beautification projects for the parks and along the streets. The association also hosts a Christmas candlelight tour of homes.

4

MIDCENTURY TO MODERN

(1950–PRESENT)

By the middle of the twentieth century, Dallas had become the nation's third-largest technology center. This growth was in part due to Jack Kilby's co-invention of the integrated circuit in 1958 while he was working at Texas Instruments. Other industries were also booming. A convention center opened downtown, and Trammel Crow and John M. Stemmons opened a mart that grew into the Dallas Market Center, the largest wholesale trade complex in the world.

The Big D saw a downtown building boom that started with the thirty-six-story First National opening at Bryan and Ervay Streets in 1954. The new six-lane Dallas–Fort Worth Turnpike (Interstate 30) opened in 1957. The State Fair of Texas was still attracting visitors from all over the world, especially in 1956, when Elvis Presley performed a legendary show at the Cotton Bowl. In 1960, the Dallas Cowboys (a.k.a. "America's Team") were granted an NFL franchise.

Dallas was among the fastest-growing Sun Belt cities, and the population soared to almost 700,000 in 1960. However, the white elite were still in charge, and business interests dominated public policy. The city was highly segregationist, with ultraconservative leadership.

Dallas of the 1960s is best known for the assassination of President John F. Kennedy on November 22, 1963. He was shot while riding in a presidential motorcade on Elm Street and was pronounced dead at Parkland Memorial Hospital, just a few blocks away from Dealey Plaza.

The Big D experienced many booms over the years. One of the most dramatic was the downtown building boom in the 1950s, which introduced many of the iconic skyscrapers still standing today. *Photograph by the author.*

Just over two hours after the assassination, Lyndon B. Johnson took the oath of office on Air Force One at Love Field.

Lee Harvey Oswald was arrested while hiding in the nearby Texas Theatre and charged with the murder. On November 24, 1963, Jack Ruby, Dallas nightclub owner, fatally shot Oswald in the basement of the Dallas Police headquarters. The shooting was broadcast live, as multiple reporters had been recording Oswald's transfer to the county jail. Oswald was taken to Parkland Memorial Hospital, where he soon died. In 1967, Ruby also died at Parkland Memorial Hospital after being transferred there from prison for lung cancer treatment.

The seven-story building at the northwest corner of Houston and Elm Streets included evidence of the shooting on the sixth floor. When the Texas School Book Depository moved out of the building in 1970, many in the community hoped the building would be torn down. Luckily, the building remained intact and was acquired by Dallas County in 1977. The Sixth Floor Museum, which chronicles the life, death and legacy of President

The "X" on Elm Street marks the location where President John F. Kennedy was assassinated. *Photograph by the author.*

Kennedy, opened on Presidents' Day in 1989. One of the exhibits is the "sniper's nest," a reconstruction of how the boxes and evidence were found near the window overlooking Dealey Plaza.

This tragic moment in American history defined Dallas for much of the country. With great care, the city has moved to embrace this significant

The Texas School Book Depository building is now the home of the Sixth Floor Museum. *Photograph by the author.*

moment in history and create opportunities to honor the legacy of the president, including the Kennedy Memorial Plaza, located a few blocks from Dealey Plaza and the Sixth Floor Museum.

However, in 1963, Dallas was labeled the "City of Hate." Dallas residents grieved with the rest of the nation, and the community knew there needed to be changes in leadership. In 1964, J. Erik Jonsson, cofounder of Texas Instruments, became mayor and worked tirelessly to improve the image and morale of the city. By 1970, he had helped transform Dallas so much that it was named an "All-American City" by *Look* magazine. In addition to many other civic accomplishments, Jonsson was instrumental in the building of Dallas/Fort Worth International Airport (DFW) in 1974. Even with the addition of DFW, Dallas was large enough to continue its support and use of Love Field.

One airline that has close ties to Love Field is Southwest Airlines, which was founded in 1966 by Dallas residents Herbert Kelleher and Rollin King. The new airline offered low-price flights within Texas with daily departures from Love Field. The first out-of-state flights started in 1979.

Southwest, which is still headquartered in Dallas, has acquired several other airlines and is now one of the largest airlines in the United States. The Frontiers of Flight Museum, located near Love Field, includes an extensive exhibition on the history of the airline. With two airports and an airline headquartered in the city, Dallas became an even more attractive location for corporate headquarters.

As the city continued to grow, so did the civil rights organizations. Residents pushed for an enlargement of the city council, and three years after the Civil Rights Act of 1964, Cleophas Anthony "C.A." Galloway was the first African American appointed as a city council member. George L. Allen became the first elected African American council member two years later and played a large role in the desegregation of Dallas's schools and public facilities. He also pushed for open housing ordinances. The George L. Allen Courts Building, located on Commerce Street, is named in his honor. When Allen resigned to take a justice of

A flag at half-mast and flowers on the grassy knoll following the assassination of President John F. Kennedy on November 22, 1963. *Courtesy of Dallas Municipal Archives.*

the peace appointment, he was replaced by Juanita Craft, distinguished NAACP leader and civil rights activist. Craft's home in South Dallas is a Dallas Landmark and is on the National Park Service's list of Historic Places of the Civil Rights Movement.

The first Hispanic council member, Anita Martinez, served from 1969 to 1973. Martinez pushed for improvements in low-income neighborhoods and assisted in opening a recreation center in West Dallas, which is named in her honor. As was the case in many U.S. cities, the 1970s and 1980s brought greater voice for all minorities. In 1978, Annette Strauss became the first woman elected as mayor of Dallas. Although the 1970s had brought another big oil and building boom to Dallas (as depicted by the glitzy image portrayed in the 1978 debut of the television show *Dallas*), Strauss's tenure occurred during the recession of the late 1980s. Oil prices plummeted, and the savings-and-loan industry collapsed, greatly impacting Dallas and its residents. Property values sharply declined, the city was still struggling with race relations and many residents moved to the suburbs.

Once again, Dallas recovered and started another boom period with the telecom industry in the 1990s. In 1993, Dallas's city council structure also greatly changed, and in 1993, the newly elected council was remarkably diverse. The city's first African American mayor, Ron Kirk, was elected in 1995 and served until 2002. The white business elite were finally starting to lose their hold on local government. The population of more than one million had a democratic government that was more responsive to the diverse constituents.

By the year 2010, the population rose to 1.2 million. That same year, the Dallas Independent School District became the eighth-largest school district in the nation, with more than 130,000 students. The downtown area experienced many revitalization programs, including great expansion of the Dallas Arts District. Klyde Warren Park created a more walkable city by connecting the downtown Dallas Arts District with Uptown Dallas. The Trinity River Corridor Project has helped build beautiful bridges and parks along the same river that attracted the first settlers.

The Big D grew quickly, always with a focus on the future. Today, it is the ninth-largest city in the United States and the third-largest in Texas. As in other cities, there have been some growing pains and tragedy. But the past is full of learning opportunities, and history teaches valuable lessons that can help guide the future.

YOUR GUIDE TO HISTORY

Margaret Hunt Hill Bridge was built in 2012 and quickly became a landmark in the bustling city that continues to grow. *Photograph by the author.*

Cavanaugh Flight Museum
North/Addison
4572 Claire Chennault, Addison
972.380.8800
www.cavflight.org
Admission charge

The Cavanaugh Flight Museum restores, operates and displays historically significant vintage aircraft. Most of the aircraft are in flyable condition and can be seen at air shows throughout the country. The museum offers rides over North Dallas in a warbird aircraft. Group rates and guided tours are available.

Dallas World Aquarium (DWA)
Downtown
1801 North Griffin Street
214.720.2224
www.dwazoo.com
Admission charge

Dallas World Aquarium (DWA) is located downtown near the Historic West End. Two adjacent warehouses, built in the early 1920s, were purchased for the venue. The interiors were completely demolished, leaving only the brick walls and support structure. The alley between both buildings became a channel between the freshwater and saltwater ecosystems on display.

One of the warehouse buildings includes Orinco, a seven-story exhibit that highlights the South American rainforest ecosystem. The Borneo features Australasian birds, fish and mammals. Outdoors, there is a year-round South African exhibit that provides close encounters with black-footed penguins and storks. There is also a traditional aquarium gallery that features coral reef and kelp forest ecosystems.

In 2004, twelve years after the aquarium opened, DWA added another area, the Mundo Maya, in a newly constructed building. Mundo Maya is the crown of DWA, with its 400,000-gallon walk-through exhibit featuring the sharks, rays and sea turtles of the Yucatan Peninsula.

The current DWA feeding schedule starts at 10:30 a.m. with the otters and ends with the sharks at 4:30 p.m. Visit the website to see the full feeding schedule, with opportunities for viewing every half hour.

FOUNDERS' PLAZA PLANE OBSERVATION AREA

Dallas/Fort Worth International Airport/Irving
1700 North Airfield Drive, Irving (exit on Highway 114 and head south on
Texan Trail to North Airfield Drive)
972.973.5270
www.dfwairport.com/founders
Free

Founders' Plaza was dedicated in 1995 as a tribute to the founders of the Dallas/Fort Worth International Airport (DFW). The plaza is small and simple and is a favorite spot for aviation enthusiasts. It is located on the north side of DFW and provides wonderful views of the aircraft coming and going.

The plaza includes telescopes, broadcasts of the control tower operators, commemorative monuments and statues. The plaza is surprisingly peaceful, with benches and a nice grassy area perfect for picnics.

Founders' Plaza Plane Observation Area at Dallas/Fort Worth Airport (DFW) is surprisingly peaceful, with benches, telescopes and statues. *Photograph by the author.*

FOUNTAIN PLACE
Downtown
1445 Ross Avenue
www.fountainplace.com
Free

Fountain Place includes the iconic glass Fountain Plaza building that has restaurants on the ground level. The exterior includes 217 small water jets designed by Dan Kiley, world-class landscape architect. This is a nice place to take a moment of rest and enjoy some peace and quiet while in the bustling Big D.

FRONTIERS OF FLIGHT MUSEUM
Northwest/Near Dallas Love Field
6911 Lemmon Avenue
214.350.3600
www.flightmuseum.com
Admission charge

George Haddaway, civil aviation icon and founder of *Flight Magazine*, donated his sizeable collection of artifacts to the University of Texas in 1963. Over the years, the collection moved to Dallas, and a nonprofit museum was established. In the 1980s, the city provided space for the museum at Love Field. Due to the collection's popularity and increasing traffic at Love Field, a larger dedicated space was needed.

In 2004, the new 100,000-square-foot facility opened near Love Field. The museum displays over thirty aircraft and space vehicles and military, commercial and general aviation artifacts. Historically important pieces are also on display, such as early fliers from the Wright brothers, artifacts from the *Hindenburg* and the *Apollo 7* spacecraft.

An excellent children's area is available and includes a child-size plane, an amphitheater, a climbing tower control structure, aviation books and hands-on-opportunities.

The museum is an affiliate of the Smithsonian Institution and draws major traveling exhibitions. The museum offers a great events calendar, classes, tours and rental options.

The Frontiers of Flight Museum was built to house the expansive collection of aviation artifacts donated by George Haddaway, a civil aviation icon and founder of *Flight Magazine*. *Photograph by the author.*

George W. Bush Presidential Center

North/Southern Methodist University (SMU)
2943 SMU Boulevard
214.200.4300
www.bushcenter.org
Admission charge

The George W. Bush Presidential Center opened in 2013. It is located on twenty-three acres on the east side of the SMU campus. The center includes permanent and rotating exhibits that explore the role of a U.S. president. The center includes a café and gift shop and is surrounded by a fifteen-acre park full of native Texas plants.

Eye by Tony Tasset is a unique downtown addition purchased by the Joule Hotel. *Courtesy of Donna Kidby.*

Giant Eyeball (*Eye*)
Downtown
1607 Main Street
Free

Just across the street from the five-star Joule Hotel is a thirty-foot-tall eyeball made of fiberglass. Outside of the eyeball being three stories tall, it is very realistic, with red veins. The eyeball was created by Tony Tasset, a Chicago-based multimedia artist who specializes in giant roadside attractions. The Joule, which has an extensive art collection, brought *Eye* to Texas in 2013.

Juanita J. Craft Civil Rights House
South
2618 Warren Avenue
214.670.3687
www.dallasculture.org
Free

Juanita J. Craft was born in 1902 in Round Rock, Texas. She moved to Dallas in 1925 and joined the National Association for the Advancement of Colored People (NAACP) in 1935. Through her work with the NAACP, Craft became an important community leader and one of the most influential civil rights advocates of the time. In 1944, Craft became the first black woman in Dallas County to vote in a public election. She played a critical role in anti-discrimination efforts in North Texas and helped organize nearly one hundred NAACP chapters. Craft was a leader in the integration efforts for Dallas universities, theaters, restaurants and the State Fair of Texas. Craft also served on the Dallas City Council from 1975 to 1979.

Despite racial tensions and multiple bombings in South Dallas, Craft moved to the Warren Avenue house that became a gathering place for young people from all over the city. Lyndon Johnson and Martin Luther King Jr. visited her modest single-story house to discuss the future of civil rights. Located in the Wheatley Place Historic District just southwest of downtown Dallas, the house is a Dallas Landmark and on the National Park Service's list of Historic Places of the Civil Rights Movement.

The house is open by appointment. Call the City of Dallas Office of Cultural Affairs office for additional information about visiting and to schedule an appointment.

The Kennedy Memorial Plaza was built as a place of reflection and remembrance. The memorial is located downtown near the Old Red Museum. *Courtesy of Donna Kidby.*

Kennedy Memorial Plaza
Downtown
646 Main Street
Free

Kennedy Memorial Plaza is located a few blocks from Dealey Plaza and the Sixth Floor Museum. It is bounded by Main, Record, Commerce and Market Streets. On June 25, 1970, the aesthetically simple monument was dedicated as a place of reflection and remembrance. Designed by noted architect Philip Johnson, the monument is meant to symbolize the freedom of President John F. Kennedy's spirit. Each year on the anniversary of President Kennedy's assassination (November 22), hundreds gather in the plaza to pay their respects.

Perot Museum of Nature and Science
Downtown
2201 North Field Street
214.428.5555
www.perotmuseum.org
Admission charge

In 2008, the five children of Margot and Ross Perot donated $50 million for a new museum in Dallas. After this donation was combined with additional fundraising efforts, the new museum opened in 2012. Named the Perot Museum of Nature and Science, the museum combined the Dallas H istory Museum (est. 1936), the Science Place (est. 1946) and the Dallas Children's Museum (est. 1995). The combination allows the museum to present a wide variety of scientific, technologic and natural history exhibits.

The museum stands fourteen stories high with over 180,000 square feet. The distinct building was designed with sustainability in mind and received four Green Globes, the highest recognition for building with minimal impact to the environment.

The facility includes eleven permanent exhibit halls and six learning labs. When entering the main lobby, visitors are immediately in awe as they see the thirty-five-foot Malawisaurus fossil. Continuing into the building, there are examples of engineering, sustainability and technology working together.

Perot Museum of Nature and Science is an award-winning immersive and interactive museum dedicated to science and nature. *Photograph by the author.*

The world-class museum has many immersive and interactive programs geared toward children but is inspiring and stimulates curiosity in guests of all ages. The museum includes a 3-D theater, café and gift shop. A wide variety of events and programs are available, including architecture tours and a speaker series.

PEROT MUSEUM OF NATURE AND SCIENCE AT FAIR PARK
East/Fair Park
3535 Grand Avenue
www.perotmuseum.org
www.fairpark.org

One of the first natural history museums in the region, the Dallas Museum of Natural History was built as part of the 1936 Texas Centennial Exhibition in Fair Park. The museum merged with two other museums and ultimately became part of the Perot Museum of Nature and Science in 2006. The Fair Park building is also now part of the Perot Museum of Nature and

Elephant statue outside the Perot Museum of Nature and Science at Fair Park. *Photograph by the author.*

Science and provides workspace for research and a home for some special collections. The building is currently closed to the public, but the exterior is a sight in and of itself.

REUNION TOWER GEO-DECK
Downtown
300 Reunion Blvd East
214.712.7040
www.reuniontower.com
Admission charge

Reunion Tower is one of the most recognizable landmarks in downtown Dallas. Built in 1978, the 561-foot tower is adjoined to the Hyatt Regency Dallas. The Geo-Deck offers unrivaled and stunning views of Dallas, and a closer look at the skyline is made possible through telescopes and cameras on the deck. Combination day and night tickets are available.

Reunion Tower, built in 1978, is one of the most recognizable landmarks in Dallas. The Geo-Deck offers stunning views of downtown landmarks, including Dealey Plaza and the Sixth Floor Museum. *Courtesy of Donna Kidby.*

Cloud Nine Café is located just above the deck. Fine dining at Five Sixty by Wolfgang Puck is located at the top, and the restaurant rotates every evening from 5:00 p.m. until closing time. The Kaleidoscope gift shop has unique Big D gifts.

SIXTH FLOOR MUSEUM AT DEALEY PLAZA
Downtown
411 Elm Street
214.747.6660
www.jfk.org
Admission charge

The seven-story building at the northwest corner of Houston and Elm Streets was built in 1901. In 1963, the building was leased by the Texas School Book Depository, a school textbook distribution firm. The building became infamous on November 22, 1963, when President John F. Kennedy

This aerial view includes Elm Street, the grassy knoll and the Texas School Book Depository building, which is now the home of the Sixth Floor Museum. *Photograph by the author.*

was assassinated. Evidence of the shooting was found on the sixth floor, and one of the depository employees, Lee Harvey Oswald, was arrested and charged with the assassination.

When the Texas School Book Depository moved out of the building in 1970, many in the community hoped the building would be torn down. Luckily, the building remained intact and was acquired by Dallas County in 1977. The building was restored, and the first five floors were used for county administration. The top two floors remained empty until the Sixth Floor Museum was opened on Presidents' Day in 1989. In 2002 (again on Presidents' Day), the museum expanded to the seventh floor.

The sixth floor includes a permanent exhibit of photographs, films and artifacts that chronicle President Kennedy's life, death and legacy. Two evidentiary areas—the sniper's nest and the storage space where a rifle was found—have been restored to their 1963 appearance. The seventh floor is home to visiting exhibits. A reading room also overlooks Dealey Plaza and includes an extensive library of books, magazines, newspapers and media.

Tickets are by timed entry in thirty-minute increments, and audio guides are provided with admission. The museum is quite busy, and it is recommended that visitors purchase tickets in advance. A museum store and café are located across the street.

St. Mark's School of Texas Planetarium and Observatory
North/Preston Hollow
10600 Preston Road
214.346.8000
www.smtexas.org
Free

St. Mark's School of Texas is a private, nonsectarian college preparatory boys' day school. It is well-known for its impressive facilities, including a planetarium, observatory and greenhouse. Planetarium events are open to the public. Check the St. Mark's Events Calendar for options.

If the schedule at St. Mark's Planetarium is limited, there is also a planetarium open to the public at the University of North Texas (UNT) in Denton. Visit www.skytheater.unt.edu for more information.

Thanks-Giving Square, located downtown, is a place dedicated to giving and living in thanks. *Photograph by the author.*

Southfork Ranch

Far North/Parker
3700 Hogge Drive, Parker
972.442.7800
www.southforkranch.com
Admission charge

Often called the "World's Most Famous Ranch," the Southfork Ranch is located in Parker, Texas. It was made famous by the Ewing family on the television series *Dallas*. Guided tours of the mansion and grounds are available and include memorabilia from the series, including the gun that shot J.R., Lucy's wedding dress and Jock's Lincoln Continental. There is a great gift shop with some very spectacular *Dallas* memorabilia that just can't be found elsewhere. Special events are held there throughout the year.

Thanks-Giving Square

Downtown
1627 Pacific Avenue
214.969.1977
www.thanksgiving.org
Free

In 1964, four local Dallas businessmen joined together in a mission to ensure Dallas was known for the heart of its citizens. They chartered the Thanks-Giving Foundation to create a public space dedicated to giving and living in thanks. After acquiring land in downtown Dallas, they built Thanks-Giving Square—a three-acre garden, chapel and museum. The garden includes sculptures and water features. The chapel welcomes all cultures and religions, and the museum includes rare historical documents related to Thanksgiving.

5

ART AND MUSEUMS

D allas has the largest urban arts district in the nation. The transformation started in the 1970s, when city officials set their minds on turning the city into a world-class arts and culture destination. In 1984, a nonprofit, the Dallas Arts District, was established to provide operational, educational and marketing support for various downtown venues.

The Dallas Arts District is located downtown and spans nineteen blocks and almost seventy acres. The area includes museums, performance halls and parks. Free festivals and activities are often held in the area. In fact, the Dallas Museum of Art, with a collection of more than twenty-four thousand works, does not charge general admission. The Crow Collection of Asian Art, located on Flora Street, also provides free admission. The Nasher Sculpture Center, which includes over three hundred pieces and an impressive collection of sculptures by Moore, Calder, Matisse and others, offers free admission the first Saturday of every month.

In addition to the beauty that can be seen indoors, the Dallas Arts District is also widely known for its architecture, with buildings designed by I.M. Pei, Renzo Piano and Norman Foster. Additionally, historic buildings such as the Belo Mansion, the Cathedral Shrine of the Virgin of Guadalupe, St. Paul United Methodist Church and Booker T. Washington High School are all located in the district. Visit www.thedallasartsdistrict. org to schedule an exterior history tour, see the special events calendar or sign up for volunteer opportunities.

The *Traveling Man* sculpture by Brad Oldham, located in Deep Ellum, is one of the many pieces of public art created by world-renowned and local Dallas artists. *Photograph by the author.*

Dallas Arts District, located downtown, spans almost seventy acres and includes a wide variety of museums and performance halls. *Photograph by the author.*

Although the downtown Dallas Arts District is an amazing destination, art can also be found in some unlikely places. The interior of the iconic Lakewood Theater in old east Dallas includes murals by the "Dallas Nine," a group of artists who were prolific during the 1930s and 1940s. Deep Ellum is home to a community-wide mural project that draws visitors from around the world. There are also three installations of the *Traveling Man*, a giant robot, in Deep Ellum. *Traveling Man* is the work of artist Brad Oldham, a world-renowned sculpture artist based in Dallas.

Great murals and sculptures can also be seen at Fair Park, including the *Tejas Warrior* above the entrance at the Hall of State building, home to the Dallas Historical Society. The buildings surrounding the Esplanade at Fair Park each include large sculptures and murals that depict the six governments that have ruled over Texas. The buildings at Fair Park, which were constructed for the Texas Centennial Exposition in 1936, make up one of the most significant art deco sites in the United States. Fair Park is also home to the African American Museum and the South Dallas Cultural Center.

Tenor and *Contralto* statues by David Newton at Fair Park. *Photograph by the author.*

Sculptures by renowned artist David Newton can also be seen at Fair Park with his recreations of Laurence Tenney Steven's original sculptures *Contralto* and *Tenor*. Newton's work can also be seen at Freedman's Cemetery, a burial ground established for Dallas's early African American population. The beautiful and powerful works were added when Dallas built a memorial in 1990 to commemorate the contributions of African Americans to the growth of the city.

Dallas is home to some unique collections, such as the Museum of Geometric and MADI Art and the Samurai Collection, both of which are located in Uptown. The Museum of Geometric and MADI Art is the only museum dedicated to MADI art in the United States, and the Samurai Collection is one of the largest museums of its kind and the only museum outside of Japan with a focus on samurai armor.

A wide array of cultural influences can be appreciated through the various art venues in the Big D. The Meadows Museum of Art, located at Southern Methodist University (SMU), contains what is considered one of the finest collections of Spanish art outside of Spain. The Latino Cultural Center, designed by renowned Mexican architect Richardo Legorreta, features Latino and Hispanic art and hosts cultural festivals. The African American Museum, located in Fair Park, includes one of the largest African American folk art collections in the United States.

Dallas has fully embraced its identity as an arts destination. The City of Dallas Office of Cultural Affairs manages many art and culture venues, including the Bath House Cultural Center at White Rock Lake, the Oak Cliff Cultural Center and the South Dallas Cultural Center. These locations and many galleries allow for viewing and the purchase of local art. There are also plenty of opportunities to partake in lectures, workshops and classes for any age. More information about the Office of Cultural Affairs and events can be found at dallasculture.org. Art&Seek, a service from KERA (NPR), provides an excellent calendar of events and artist spotlights that can be found at artandseek.org.

YOUR GUIDE TO HISTORY

The powerful statues by David Newton at Freedman's Cemetery commemorate what is one of the largest freedman cemeteries in the country. *Courtesy of Donna Kidby.*

African American Museum
East/Fair Park
3536 Grand Avenue
214.565.9026
www.aamdallas.org
Free

In 1881, the Bishop Home Mission Society founded Bishop College in Marshall, Texas, to serve black students living in east Texas. Bishop College moved to Dallas in 1961 in an effort to attract more students. The African American Museum was originally part of the college's special collections and was started in 1974. The museum started operating independently in 1979. Private donations and a Dallas city bond helped secure a new facility for the museum.

The current museum is located in Fair Park and occupies the same site as the Texas Centennial Exposition's Hall of Negro Life. Built in the shape of a cross, the 38,000-square-foot structure is home to a rich assortment of African American art and items related to African American history. The museum includes four vaulted galleries, a theater, a research library, a studio arts area, classrooms and a sculpture garden. The permanent collections include African art, African American fine art, magazines and historical and political archives.

The African American Museum is home to one of the largest African American folk art collections in the United States and features works by Clementine Hunter, David Butler, George White, Mose Tolliver, Sister Gertrude Morgan, Bessie Harvey and Willard "The Texas Kid" Watson.

Lectures and special events are held often at the museum. Guided and group tours are available.

The Ann and Gabriel Barbier-Mueller Museum: The Samurai Collection
Uptown/Near Victory Park
2501 North Harwood Street
214.965.1032
www.samuraicollection.org
Free

The Barbier-Mueller family includes four generations of art collectors. Joseph Mueller, born in 1887 in Switzerland, became one of the greatest art collectors of all time. His passion for art started in his youth, and he is well-known for spending his entire annual income to buy Ferdinand Hodler's *Die Liebe* at age twenty-two.

In 1955, Joseph's daughter Monique married Jean Paul Barbier, a collector in his own right. In 1977, three months after Joseph's passing, Jean Paul helped open the first Barbier-Mueller Museum in Geneva. The family opened additional museums in Europe and South Africa and started the Friends of the Barbier-Mueller Museum Association, which now has thousands of members.

Soon after the Barbier-Mueller Museum opened, Monique and Jean Paul's oldest son, Jean Gabriel, set out traveling to find acquisitions. Gabriel came to Dallas on a tour with the Modern Museum of Art's International Committee. He was hooked on the city, and in 1979, he moved to Dallas in pursuit of a career in real estate. Today, Gabriel is the CEO of Harwood International, a development firm that owns sixteen blocks of Uptown; much of the walkable transformation of Uptown can be traced back to his vision of a greener city.

The collector's gene was passed on to Gabriel. Together with his wife, Ann, he established the Samurai Collection in 2012 to house the couple's ever-expanding collection of Japanese armor.

The museum is one of the largest museums of its kind and the only museum outside of Japan with a focus on samurai armor. The collection includes over one thousand objects. The armor, suits, helmets, masks and weaponry are rotated twice annually.

The museum is located above the Saint Ann Restaurant. Complimentary valet parking is located at Harwood and Moody Streets across from the St. Ann's School building.

Bath House Cultural Center
East/White Rock Lake
521 East Lawther Drive
214.670.8749
www.dallasculture.org
Free

One of the first uses of art deco architecture in the Southwest, the Bath House Cultural Center building is a gem situated on the east shores of White Rock Lake. This Dallas landmark was influenced by the Paris Exposition of

One of the first examples of art deco architecture in the Southwest, the Bath House Cultural Center building is a gem situated on the east shores of White Rock Lake. *Courtesy of Donna Kidby.*

1925. Originally known as the Municipal Bath House, it was built in 1930 and provided lockers, changing rooms and concessions for those who came to swim at the lake.

In 1953, the city of Dallas started to use the lake as a water supply, and swimming was prohibited. The building sat vacant for the next twenty-five years. After art activists urged the City of Dallas to restore the building, it opened to the public as the city's first neighborhood cultural center in 1981.

The center serves as a venue for local artists and independent theater. Over twenty art exhibits rotate through the center per year, and the 120-seat theater hosts a variety of performances. The center also presents concerts, festivals, lectures and workshops. The White Rock Lake Museum, located in the center, opened in 2004 and provides information on the park's natural and cultural history.

CROW COLLECTION OF ASIAN ART
Downtown
2010 Flora Street
214.979.6440
www.crowcollection.org
Free

Fred Trammell Crow was born in Dallas in 1914. He was the fifth out of eight children reared in a three-room house in East Dallas. He grew up working odd jobs, including cleaning bricks and plucking chickens. He attended Woodrow Wilson High School, the only high school in east Dallas at the time. After his graduation, he attended Southern Methodist University (SMU) and obtained a CPA at the age of twenty-four. He joined the U.S. Navy, and when he returned to Dallas a few years after World War II, he saw great opportunity for growth in the city.

In 1948, Crow built his first warehouse in Dallas. He continued to build and lease warehouses along the Trinity River and quickly became one of the most prolific warehouse builders in Dallas. He diversified and started to erect office buildings, industrial parks, garages and, eventually, high-rises. By 1970, he was building on a national level, and his skyscrapers reshaped cities throughout the United States.

Along his path to becoming a real estate giant, Crow and his wife, Margaret, started collecting Asian art. In 1998, he and Margaret founded the Trammel and Margaret Crow Collection of Asian Art and donated 598 pieces of their extensive collection.

The museum was and still is free to the public, as the Crows wanted to share their love of Asian art and culture with the city they helped develop. Today, the collection includes permanent galleries dedicated to the art of China, Japan, India and Southeast Asia. The museum also showcases traveling exhibits and hosts community events, seminars and workshops. The center is surrounded by a lush sculpture garden.

The Crow Collection of Asian Art was established when Trammel and Margaret Crow donated their extensive Asian art collection. *Courtesy of Donna Kidby.*

Dallas Museum of Art
Downtown
1717 North Harwood
214.922.1200
www.dma.org
Free (except special events and exhibits)

The Dallas Museum of Art (DMA) celebrated its one-hundred-year anniversary in 2003. The original home of the DMA was in the Public Library, with an admission fee of twenty-five cents. In 1909, the already celebrated museum moved to Fair Park, and the Dallas Arts Association officially donated the permanent collection and management of the museum to the City of Dallas.

Over the years, the collection and special exhibits have been on display at the Adolphus Hotel, Majestic Theatre and on the ninth floor of the Dallas Power and Light Company building. A new museum opened at Fair Park in 1936, when the Centennial Exposition drew over 154,000 visitors.

The Dallas Museum of Art provides free general admission for the public to view a collection of over twenty-four thousand works spanning five thousand years. *Photograph by the author.*

The museum moved downtown in 1984 and is now one of the top ten largest art museums in the country. The global collection includes more than twenty-four thousand works spanning over five thousand years of history. The museum also houses contemporary collections and hosts traveling expeditions.

Educational programs, lectures, workshops, concerts and festivals are held often at DMA. The museum also hosts evening events and programs. Food is available at the DMA Café, and there is a museum store. All public galleries and restrooms are ADA accessible. Late-night events and special exhibits require an admission fee.

The Museum of Geometric and MADI Art
Uptown
3109 Carlisle Street
214.855.7802
www.geometricmadimuseum.org
Free

Kilgore & Kilgore is one of the oldest law firms in Dallas. The firm started by representing oil and gas businesses. Today, the firm is owned by Bill Masterson. Bill and his wife, Dorothy, are lifelong art collectors and decided to open a museum to house their extensive MADI collection.

MADI stands for "Movement, Abstraction, Dimension and Invention." Carmelo Arden Quin articulated the ideas of the MADI movement in his *MADI Manifesto* (Buenos Aires, 1946). Bill and Dorothy Masterson were introduced to Quin and other MADI artists while traveling the world. Artists from Europe, Russia, Japan, South America and the United States are represented in the museum. The Museum of Geometric and MADI Art is the only museum in the United States with its primary focus on MADI art.

Goss-Michael Foundation
Northwest of downtown
1405 Turtle Creek Boulevard
214.696.0555
www.gossmichaelfoundation.org
Free

The Goss-Michael Foundation is dedicated to contributing to Dallas's art community. Stimulating exhibits are rotated on a quarterly basis throughout the year. The foundation also has a resource center available for use by aspiring young artists and offers a scholarship program.

Watch the site for special events, such as Saturday Sketch days. Be sure to check the schedule for Family Fundays, which are regularly held on the weekends. Fundays give parents and children a chance to co-create art projects, using gallery exhibitions as inspiration.

Latino Cultural Center
Downtown
2600 Live Oak Street
214.671.0045
www.lcc.dallasculture.org
Free

A division of the City of Dallas Office of Cultural Affairs, the Latin Cultural Center (LCC) serves to promote, preserve and develop Latino and Hispanic arts and culture. The building was designed by renowned Mexican architect Richardo Legorreta, and the center's doors opened in 2003. The 27,000-square-foot facility includes two visual art galleries, a 300-seat theater, a sculpture courtyard and a large outdoor plaza.

The Latino Cultural Center was designed by renowned Mexican architect Richardo Legorreta. *Courtesy of Donna Kidby.*

Year-round programing includes visual arts exhibits, film screenings, music performances and theater productions. Workshops, lectures and camps are available. The expansive courtyard is often used for cultural festivals, including Dieciseis de Septiembre to Las Posadas.

Tours are available and free, but reservations must be made four weeks in advance. Contact LCC for reservations and additional group opportunities.

MEADOWS MUSEUM OF ART
North of Highland Park
5900 Bishop Boulevard
214.768.2516
www.meadowsmuseumdallas.org
Admission charge

In 1936, Algur Hurtle Meadows and his friend Ralph G. Trippett partnered with J.W. Gilliland to form the General American Oil Company. Headquartered in Dallas, the firm grew rapidly and acquired many oil-producing properties.

In the 1950s, business took Meadows to Spain, where he was greatly inspired by his visit to the Prado Museum in Madrid. This inspiration turned into a passion for collecting. In 1961, Meadows's wife, Virginia, passed away. He donated a large collection of Spanish art to Southern Methodist University (SMU) in her memory. As his collecting expanded to French Impressionists and post-Impressionists, so did his philanthropy. In 1965, he donated a large collection to SMU and enough funds to turn the former administration building into an art gallery. The Meadows Museum of Art opened on the SMU campus in 1975.

After Meadows passed away in 1978, the Meadows Foundation continued to generously support the growth and expansion of the extraordinary collection. Today, the Meadows Museum of Art houses one of the finest collections of Spanish art outside of Spain. The four major collections include early Renaissance to modern works and cover thousands of years of Spanish culture. The museum includes a plaza and sculpture garden. Tour programs, lectures, special exhibits, drawing classes and concerts are offered. Admission is complimentary on Thursdays after 5:00 p.m.

Nasher Sculpture Center
Downtown
2001 Flora Street
214.242.5100
www.nashersculpturecenter.org
Admission charge

Raymond Nasher, a banker and developer of commercial and retail space, moved to Dallas in 1950. He also served in multiple government positions, including as a delegate to the United Nations and on President George Bush's Committee on the Arts and Humanities.

Raymond and his wife, Patsy, started their sculpture collection in the 1950s when traveling in Mexico. Their collection started to grow rapidly in the 1970s and 1980s, as Raymond became one of the first developers to include art in his commercial building developments. By the 1990s, the assemblage was regarded as the world's finest collection of modern and contemporary sculpture in private hands.

The Nashers never felt art should be locked behind closed doors and generously shared pieces to display in prominent museums like the Guggenheim in New York, the National Gallery of Art in Washington and the Dallas Museum of Art. Many of these museums courted Nasher, hoping to provide a permanent home for the collection.

Nasher eventually decided to build his own museum and spent $70 million of his fortune to build the Nasher Sculpture Center. The center was designed by Renzo Piano and Peter Walker. It opened in 2003 in the heart of the Dallas Arts District. The 55,000-square-foot interior blends perfectly with the two-acre sculpture garden. The center has over three hundred pieces in the impressive collection and includes masterpieces by Moore, Calder, Rodin, Matisse and others.

Special exhibits, concerts and outdoor movies are planned throughout the year. Admission is free the first Saturday of each month.

Oak Cliff Cultural Center

Southwest of Downtown/Oak Cliff
223 West Jefferson Boulevard
214.670.3777
dallasculture.org
Free

Oak Cliff is one of Dallas's oldest neighborhoods, and in 2010, the City of Dallas Office of Cultural Affairs opened the Oak Cliff Cultural Center to serve the community. The center hosts workshops, music and dance classes, camps and cultural festivals. The center also provides a venue for local artists and rotating exhibits throughout the year.

South Dallas Cultural Center

East/Fair Park at the Southern Gate
3400 South Fitzhugh Avenue
214.939.2787
dallasculture.org
Free

Created in 1982 and renovated in 2007, the South Dallas Cultural Center provides a multipurpose art facility across from Fair Park. The center includes a 120-seat theater, a visual arts gallery and studios for dance, printmaking, digital recording and photography. The center also provides a venue for local artists, and exhibits are rotated throughout the year.

Texas Sculpture Garden

Far North/Frisco
6801 Gaylord Parkway, Frisco
www.texassculpturegarden.org
Free

The Texas Sculpture Garden was built to celebrate and display the work of local Texas artists. The interior collection is inside the lobby of HALL Park in Frisco. The exterior sculptures are on display among winding trails with a lake and fountains that complement the work.

6

MUSIC AND THEATER

Given the size and diversity of Dallas, it is no surprise that the city has a rich and varied history when it comes to music and theater. Fair Park, Deep Ellum and the various cultural centers and locally owned venues throughout the city provide plenty of options. In addition, the Moody Performance Hall, AT&T Performing Arts Center, Winspear Opera House, Meyerson Symphony Center and Wyly Theater are all located within the Dallas Arts District. These beautifully designed performing arts centers provide a home for many local companies and host touring companies that represent all disciplines.

The Winspear Opera House, on Flora Street, was designed by Norman Foster, a Pritzker Prize–winning architect, and has been recognized as one of the finest opera houses in the country. The Winspear is the main venue for the Dallas Opera, which was founded in 1957. The opera offers public simulcasts of opening night, with free outdoor viewing on the great lawn at Klyde Warren Park.

Nearby, the Meyerson Symphony Center was designed by architect I.M. Pei, another Pritzker Prize–winning architect, in partnership with acoustician Russell Johnson. Built in 2006, it serves as the home to the Dallas Symphony Orchestra (DSO), which started in 1900. Over the years, DSO has performed abroad and received numerous accolades and recording contracts. The official children's chorus of the DSO, the Children's Chorus of Greater Dallas (CCGD), is one of the largest and most prestigious youth choral programs in America.

Deep Ellum is just northeast of downtown and was started as a freedmen's town in the late 1800s. By the 1920s, the area had become a hotbed for blues and early jazz and provided a stage for many musicians, including T-Bone Walker. *Photograph by the author.*

Although the classical influence is strong in Dallas, when it comes to music, the city is probably best known for blues and country greats with ties to Deep Ellum. Deep Ellum is just northeast of downtown and was started as a freedmen's town in the late 1800s. By the 1920s, the area had become a hotbed for blues and early jazz. Although Deep Ellum still provides a lively blues and country scene, there are plenty of musical options to suite any taste.

Dallas has also been home to many musicians. Aaron Thibeaux "T-Bone" Walker started his musical career as a teenager in South Dallas. After leaving school at age ten, he was a professional performer on the blues circuit by age fifteen. His innovative style influenced greats like B.B. King, Ray Charles, Chuck Berry and Jimi Hendrix. Walker's style also greatly influenced Dallas, which developed its own rich R&B culture in the 1950s.

A central part of this scene was the American Woodman Hall, located in South Dallas at the corner of Oakland and Carpenter Streets. Sunday afternoon shows were packed with both white and black people who came together during this segregated time for the love of music. Young musicians got their feet wet, and more experienced musicians often sat in or led the bands.

One of the more experienced musicians who sat in at the Woodman was Ray Charles, who had moved to Dallas in the mid-1950s due to its central location. He lived with his wife and newborn son, Ray Jr., at their small bungalow at 2642 Eugene Street in South Dallas. While in Dallas, he had some hits, like "I Got a Woman" and "Hallelujah I Love Her So," but he was still struggling and on the road touring most of the time. Charles and his family only had a brief stay in Dallas and moved to Los Angeles in 1958.

Additional musicians, such as the D.O.C., Lisa Loeb, Vanilla Ice, Meat Loaf, the Reverend Horton Heat, the Dixie Chicks and the Old 97s all have strong connections to the Big D. Booker T. Washington High School, located in the Dallas Arts District, transitioned into a performing and visual arts magnet school in the 1970s. Alumni of the school include Edie Brickell, Erykah Badu, jazz trumpeter Roy Hargrove and cellist John Koen.

Another famous musical star was born and raised in Dallas but dropped out of school before graduating. Like T-Bone Walker, Stevie Ray Vaughan was born and raised in Oak Cliff. Vaughan, who dropped out of high school at seventeen, released his debut album, *Texas Flood*, in 1983 and sold over a half-million copies. He also played on the 1983 *Let's Dance* album with David Bowie. He headlined tours with Jeff Beck and Joe Cocker. Sadly, he died in a helicopter crash when he was thirty-five and is buried at the Laurel Land Memorial Park in Dallas.

Dallas has also been or is home to many famous actors. Morgan Fairchild and Robin Wright were both born in Dallas. Ashley and Jessica Simpson were both raised in Richardson, a suburb of Dallas. Luke and Owen Wilson both attended St. Mark's, a private preparatory school for boys in Dallas, and their father, Bob Wilson, helped pioneer Dallas's public television affiliate. The list of famous performers could go on, as there are plenty of talents who were born or raised in Dallas.

The long history of performance in Dallas and the wide variety of venues will ensure you can find entertainment regardless of your musical or theatrical interests. If you are looking for a more playful evening, try the Pocket Sandwich Theatre, where you can throw popcorn at the actors. If you need to entertain the whole family, try the Dallas Children's Theater. Looking for something local or hip? Check the concert lineups at venues in Deep Ellum (deepellumtexas.com) or one of the cultural centers operated by the City of Dallas (dallasculture.org). Art&Seek, a service from KERA (NPR), provides an excellent calendar of events that can be found at artandseek.org.

If you are looking to see a motion picture, why not head to the Texas Theatre, which has been open since 1931 and made national news when Lee Harvey Oswald was arrested there after the assassination of President John F. Kennedy in 1963.

YOUR GUIDE TO HISTORY

The Majestic Theatre opened as a vaudeville theater in 1921. The theater still serves as a performing arts venue. *Photograph by the author.*

Anita N. Martinez Ballet Folkorico
East
422 Live Oak Street
214.828.0181
www.anmbf.org

Anita N. Martinez is a fifth-generation Texan and Mexican American born in Dallas. She was raised in the community known as Little Mexico and was very active in her community. She became the first Hispanic person elected to serve as a Dallas City Council member in 1969 and the first Hispanic woman elected to the city council of a major U.S. city.

In 1975, she helped open a recreation center in the economically depressed west side of town. The center is named in her honor, and it was here that she started the Anita N. Martinez Ballet Folkorico (ANMBF) with the goal of impacting Hispanic youth by providing opportunities to learn about Hispanic culture. The study and practice of the traditional dances of Mexico also resulted in enhanced cultural awareness and pride in heritage.

By 1990, ANMBF had held its first season with professional dancers trained in Mexico. Today, ANMBF continues to showcase professional performances at various venues throughout Dallas. The foundation also includes a wide array of educational opportunities, youth programs and camps that encourage historical and cultural knowledge.

The Black Academy of Arts and Letters
Downtown/Dallas Convention Center Theatre Complex
1309 Canton Street
214.743.2400
www.tbaal.org

The Black Academy of Arts and Letters (TBAAL) is dedicated to creating awareness of black artistic accomplishments and supporting young artists. Originally named the Junior Black Academy of Arts and Letters, the organization was founded by Curtis King in 1977.

Housed downtown in the Dallas Convention Center, it is the nation's only arts institution and African American organization housed in a major urban convention center. Annually, TBAAL presents over one hundred programs in theater, music, dance, literary arts, film and visual art. In addition, TBAAL provides educational programs and workshops.

Cara Mía Theatre Company
214.516.0706
www.caramiatheatre.org

The Cara Mía Theatre Company was started in 1996 and quickly filled the void for a theater company that focuses on the Mexican American experience. Using theater, literature and education programs, the nonprofit company broadens the understanding of Chicano and Latino culture. Season information is available online, and performances are available throughout the year at various venues locally and nationally.

Children's Chorus of Greater Dallas
400 North St. Paul Street, Suite 510
214.965.0491
www.thechildrenschorus.org

Founded in 1996, the Children's Chorus of Greater Dallas (CCGD) is the official children's chorus of the Dallas Symphony Orchestra (DSO). The five hundred children and teenagers in grades four through twelve make CCGD one of the largest and most prestigious youth choral programs in America. The CCGD's Deloitte Concert Series is presented at the Meyerson Symphony Center, and ancillary community performances are presented in a variety of performance halls throughout Dallas. Check the CCGD website to learn more about upcoming performances or purchase tickets.

Dallas Black Dance Theatre
Downtown
2700 Ann Williams Way
214.871.2376
www.dbdt.com

Dallas Black Dance Theatre is the oldest continuously operating professional dance company in Dallas. The company consists of professional, full-time dancers performing a mixed repertory of contemporary modern dance. Watch the events calendar for the performance schedule. The Dee and Charles Wyly Theatre, located in downtown Dallas, is the company's home performance venue.

Dallas Children's Theater
Northeast/Rosewood Center
5938 Skillman Street
214.740.0051
www.dct.org

Dallas Children's Theater (DCT) always has an amazing lineup of performances, with classic storybooks brought to life on stage, holiday favorites and special family-friendly premieres. Located in northeast Dallas, DCT features performances that often include after-show options with activities, treats, games and giveaways. Check the performance listing for options and age recommendations.

The Dallas Opera
Downtown/Margot and Bill Winspear Opera House
2403 Flora Street
214.443.1042
www.dallasopera.org

The Dallas Opera, which was officially founded in 1957, provides outstanding mainstage and chamber opera at the Margot and Bill Winspear Opera House located in the Dallas Arts District. Winspear Opera House was designed by Norman Foster, a Pritzker Prize–winning architect, and has been recognized as one of America's finest opera houses. The opera also provides free public simulcasts on opening night, and the public can watch free opera under the stars on the great lawn at Klyde Warren Park.

Dallas Summer Musicals
201.421.5678
www.dallassummermusicals.org

Dallas Summer Musicals (DSM) started in 1941 at Fair Park as Opera Under the Stars. When air-conditioning was installed in the Music Hall at Fair Park in 1951, the performances moved indoors, and the name changed to State Fair Musicals. The indoor venue offered more comfort for the audience and greater creativity when staging the performances. Stars like Jack Benny, Debbie Reynolds, Judy Garland and Carol Burnett packed the house. Performances staged by top musical directors and choreographers were not uncommon.

In 1962, another name change came when the organization became a civic organization. Dallas Summer Musicals (DSM) is a now a nonprofit that promotes musical theater, bringing Broadway to Dallas, and presents shows at various venues throughout North Texas, including the Music Hall. DSM also invests in the Dallas community through scholarships, complimentary performances and education.

Dallas Symphony Orchestra
Downtown/Meyerson Symphony Center
2301 Flora Street
214.849.4376
www.mydso.com

The Dallas Symphony Orchestra (DSO) has grown with the city. It started in 1900, when a group of forty musicians gave a concert at Turner Hall. By 1945, the group had transformed into a full professional orchestra under conductor Antal Dorati. Over the years, DSO has presented abroad and received numerous accolades and record contracts. DSO primarily presents at the Meyerson Symphony Center in the Dallas Arts District. Season or single tickets are available, and some community concerts are free to the public.

Dallas Theater Center
Downtown
2400 Flora Street
214.880.0202
www.dallastheatercenter.org

The Dallas Theater Center (DTC) is one of the leading regional theaters in the country and performs at the AT&T Performing Center and the Wyly Theater in the Dallas Arts District. Additional performances are held at the Kalita Humphreys Theater, the only freestanding theater designed and built by Frank Lloyd Wright. Founded in 1959, the DTC was one of the first regional theaters in the United States and has become one of the leaders in producing experimental interpretations of classics.

DALLAS WINDS
214.565.9463
www.dallaswinds.org

The Dallas Winds debuted in 1985 and includes a combination of woodwind, brass and percussion players who perform an eclectic blend of musical styles. The group's home venue is the Morton H. Meyerson Concert Center. Summer concerts are performed at the historic Fair Park Bandshell in Fair Park.

Dallas Winds has created multiple recordings, garnered numerous accolades and can often be heard on the *Performance Today* radio program.

FINE ARTS CHAMBER PLAYERS (FACP)
Design District/Northwest of Downtown
Sammons Center for the Arts
3630 Harry Hines Boulevard, Suite 302
214.520.2219
www.fineartschamberplayers.org
Free

Founded in 1981, the Fine Arts Chamber Players (FACP) provides free concerts of classical music. Most concerts are performed at the Horchow Auditorium in the Dallas Museum of Art located in the Dallas Arts District on Harwood Street.

LAKEWOOD THEATER
East
1825 Abrams Road

Located in one of the oldest suburban shopping areas in Dallas, the art deco Lakewood Theater and its iconic one-hundred-foot neon sign are well-known landmarks in East Dallas. The Lakewood Theater opened in 1938, and unlike many other theaters of the time, it was not meant for vaudeville acts but for motion pictures. The opening film was *Love Finds Andy Hardy*, starring Mickey Rooney, Judy Garland and Lana Turner. The theater closed in 2015 and reopened as a Bowlski's bowling alley. The new owners have preserved many of the murals, original tiles and the stage with plans to occasionally host live acts and karaoke.

Located in East Dallas, the Lakewood Theater is another fabulous art deco icon. *Photograph by the author.*

MAJESTIC THEATRE
Downtown
1925 Elm Street
214.670.3687
www.dallasculture.org

Located in the heart of downtown at the corner of Elm and Harwood Streets, the Majestic Theatre opened on April 21, 1921, as a vaudeville theater. At the time of its opening, this area of downtown was known as Theater Row, but the Majestic is the last survivor.

By the 1930s, the vaudeville era was coming to an end, and the theater started to present movies. The last movie was shown in 1973, then the theater closed. The Hoblitzelle Foundation gifted the theater to the City of Dallas in 1976. In 1983, it reopened after a major restoration and is now a performing arts venue managed by the City of Dallas Office of Cultural Affairs.

METROPOLITAN WINDS
972.680.4444
www.metropolitanwinds.org

The Metropolitan Winds was founded in 1993 and consists of members who are professional musicians, band directors and private music teachers. Performances showcase a wide repertoire and are held throughout the community, including regular performances at the Dallas City Performance Hall in the Dallas Arts District on Flora Street.

MORTON H. MEYERSON SYMPHONY CENTER
Downtown
2301 Flora Street
214.670.3600
www.dallasculture.org

The Meyerson Symphony Center opened in 1989, when it was apparent that Dallas needed a major facility for cultural events. The beautiful building was designed by architect I.M. Pei in partnership with acoustician Russell Johnson. The sophisticated space is optimal for concerts and serves as the main performance hall for the Dallas Symphony Orchestra (DSO).

Music Hall at Fair Park

East/Fair Park
909 First Avenue
214.565.1116
www.liveatthemusichall.com

Like most of Fair Park, the Music Hall building was constructed in preparation for the Texas Centennial Exposition of 1936. At the time, the hall was called the Fair Park Auditorium and was dedicated "to the good, the true, and the beautiful." The theatrical debut was on October 10, 1925, with the musical premiere of Sigmund Romberg's *The Student Prince*.

Eventually, the name was changed to the Music Hall, and the Crystal Terrace Restaurant became M Dining. Luckily, the transformation and renovations have preserved the Spanish Baroque style hall.

Over the years, the Music Hall has served as a home for the Dallas Opera, Dallas Symphony and Fort Worth Dallas Ballet. Today, it hosts large- and small-scale public and private functions and is a nationally recognized venue for Broadway musicals, grand operas, concerts and pageants.

Pocket Sandwich Theatre

North/Mockingbird Central Plaza
5400 East Mockingbird Lane
214.821.1860
www.pocketsandwich.com

Pocket Sandwich Theatre started in 1980 and is the second-longest continually operating theater in Dallas. The company performs "entertainment" theater—mainly comedies and melodramas. Pocket Theatre is a dinner theater, although food and beverage service is optional. The company provides a friendly, casual atmosphere and offers a fifty-cent basket of popcorn to throw at the actors. Reservations are recommended and can be made online.

Shakespeare Dallas
Downtown/Samuell Grand Park: 1500 Tenison Parkway
North/Addison Circle Park: 4970 Addison Circle
214.559.2778
www.shakespearedallas.org

This program started in 1971 with a one-man version of *Hamlet*. The tradition grew over the years. Now, Shakespeare Dallas provides community enrichment and educational programs and multiple productions per season. The year-round performances are held at Addison Circle Park and downtown at the Samuell Grand Park, allowing patrons to experience Shakespeare in a casual park setting. Additional educational programs and indoor winter performances are available. Check the website for availability and locations.

SMU Meadows School of the Arts
North/Southern Methodist University (SMU)
6101 Bishop Boulevard
214.768.2000
www.smu.edu

Southern Methodist University (SMU) Meadows School of the Arts provides a robust performing arts season, including student performances and recitals. The ticket office is in the lobby of the Greer Garson Theatre. Tickets can also be purchased one hour prior to performances at the Bob Hope Theatre or Caruth Auditorium. Performance options and times are available online.

Texas Ballet
North/Richardson
670 North Coit Road, Suite 2379, Richardson
214.377.8576
www.texasballettheater.org

Texas Ballet has spent more than fifty years providing creative and expressive performances in various venues throughout Dallas and Fort Worth. The company creates and presents classical and cutting-edge ballet that is accessible to all ages. The online calendar provides information about upcoming performances and links to purchase tickets online.

TEXAS THEATRE

Southwest
231 West Jefferson Boulevard
214.948.1546
www.thetexastheatre.com

Texas Theatre opened in 1931. It was the first theater in Dallas with air conditioning and operated until 1989. It became world-famous in 1963, when Lee Harvey Oswald tried to hide out there after the assassination of President John F. Kennedy. Oswald was spotted by a concessions employee and quickly arrested.

The theater was almost demolished in the 1990s, but it was saved by the Oak Cliff Foundation, and the theater still operates today.

7

PARKS, RECREATION AND NATURE PRESERVES

When it comes to parks, recreation and natural areas, Dallas has greatly benefited from the forethought of some early residents. Even during the early boomtown years, natural space was recognized as an important need in a growing town, and groups like the Dallas Federation of Women's Clubs played a critical role in promoting health and leisure within the city. Land was graciously donated by some of the earliest settlers to be used for recreation, and some of the earliest neighborhoods developed on the outskirts of the burgeoning city included large green space allotments for the residents.

Today, the Dallas Parks and Recreation System is one of the largest municipal park systems in the United States. The city manages almost four hundred parks with over twenty thousand acres of developed and preserved land. Dallas is well-known by avid bicyclers and joggers, with over 150 miles of trails. Although there are plenty of purely natural settings, many of the earlier parks were influenced by the City Beautiful Movement that flourished at the start of the twentieth century.

George Kessler, one of Dallas's prominent urban planners, was a large advocate of the movement that promoted tree-lined walkways, fountains and public art incorporated into natural settings. His influence can be seen at Fair Park and throughout the city, as he provided the Kessler Plan to the city in 1909. The Kessler Plan included approaches to prevent flooding from the Trinity River and improve congestion downtown. One of the best impacts of the urban planning of the time was the goal to have every neighborhood within walking distance of a park.

The City of Dallas manages almost four hundred parks containing over twenty thousand acres of land. Pictured are the swans at Fair Park, home of the State Fair of Texas. *Photograph by the author.*

Many parks include water features to help people cool down during the summer months, and some of the parks include man-made lakes that were originally created to provide a water source for the city. Bachman Lake, near Love Field, was built in 1903 as a water source. It was soon found to be too small to provide water for the ever-growing city and was replaced by White Rock Lake by 1911. The city also quickly outgrew this water resource. Wisely, the city purchased additional land surrounding both of these lakes and repurposed the lakes and surrounding land for recreation. White Rock Lake, which officially became a park in 1929, includes 1,015 acres and is wildly popular.

White Rock Lake also provides evidence of the impact of President Franklin D. Roosevelt's New Deal projects in the city. The Civilian Conservation Corps (CCC) had a camp at White Rock Lake and provided training and education to young men from 1935 to 1942. A statue at the park honors the 3,000 CCC workers and their efforts at the park, including planting 1,500 trees and building overlooks, pavilions and recreation buildings. Other CCC and Civil Works Administration (CWA) projects were not as grand but made great improvements in local parks, and markers can be seen at additional parks and green spaces throughout town, such as Dealey Plaza.

The names of the parks also reveal much of the city's history and the impact of its citizens. Dealey Plaza was named in honor of George Bannerman Dealey, publisher of the *Dallas Morning News*, which debuted in 1885. Griggs Park, in the Uptown area, is named after Reverend Allen Griggs, a former slave who helped establish Texas's first black newspaper and the first black high school in Texas. Reverchon Park, located on Maple Avenue in modern-day Uptown, was named after Julien Reverchon, a well-known botanist and one of the La Reunion settlers. Additional parks and centers are named after community members who served in government, such as the Anita N. Martinez and Juanita Craft Recreation Centers. A full listing of Dallas Parks and Recreation centers can be found at www.dallasparks.org.

Dallas parks range from large nature preserves to quirky and quiet gems nestled in the bustling city. Dragon Park, a privately owned space that is open to the public, is slightly hidden on Cedar Springs Road. Upon entering, you find yourself in a tranquil space with unique statues and beautiful foliage. Although small, the space is incredibly peaceful.

You can't get lost in Dragon Park, but you definitely could in the Great Trinity Forest. Containing a combined six thousand acres of grassland, forest land and acres of management strands, Great Trinity Forest is the largest urban bottomland hardwood forest in the United States and the largest forest within city limits. It supports a variety of plant and animal species, including over sixty resident bird species and two hundred migrant species that pass through on the journey between Canada and Mexico. The Trinity River Audubon Center is the gateway to the forest, providing a beautiful educational center and miles of nature trails, gardens and more.

Along with the Trinity River Audubon Center, Dallas is well-known for the Dallas Arboretum and Botanical Gardens. The sixty-six acres on the eastern shore of White Rock Lake opened to the public as a botanical garden in 1984 and is ranked one of the best in the nation. There are multiple themed areas planned to provide a vibrant display of color regardless of the season.

Just north of Dallas, Farmers Branch, where many of the early Peters Colony settlers lived, also provides a wealth of gardens. The area was selected by the settlers for its fertile soil and access to water. Most notably, the town—the motto of which is "City in a Park"—has over 1,500 rosebushes, with over 500 varieties in the many parks lining the creeks that pass through the town.

YOUR GUIDE TO HISTORY

A trail man, part of the *Cattle Drive* sculptures at Pioneer Plaza. *Courtesy of Donna Kidby.*

Bachman Lake/Bachman Lake Trail
Northwest/Near Love Field
3500 Northwest Highway
www.dallascounty.org
Free

Bachman Lake is a 205-acre stocked freshwater lake just north of Love Field. The lake was built in 1903 by damming Backman Branch, a Trinity River tributary. It was soon found to be too small to provide water for the ever-growing Dallas and was replaced by White Rock Lake by 1911.

A three-and-a-half-mile (5K) trail includes sixteen exercise stations, benches and water fountains along the way. The park is also home to picnic areas, a pavilion, a recreation center and an indoor aquatic center. There is a restroom on the south side. Parking is available on Bachman Drive.

Cedar Ridge Preserve
Far Southwest
7171 Mountain Creek Parkway
972.709.7784
www.audubondallas.org/cedar-ridge-preserve
Free (donations appreciated)

Cedar Ridge Preserve is six hundred acres jointly owned by Dallas County and the City of Dallas. The preserve is located about twenty miles southwest of downtown Dallas and provides a mix of blackland prairie, limestone escarpment and Hill Country–type terrain. There are great views and heavily wooded areas.

Audubon Dallas provides maintenance, education, lectures, guided walks and volunteer opportunities. The preserve includes classrooms, picnic tables, an outdoor amphitheater, butterfly gardens and over eight miles of nature trails. Trail maps are available on the preserve's website.

BECKERT PARK
North/Addison
5044 Addison Circle Drive, Addison
972.450.2851
www.addisontx.gov
Free

Located between Quorum Drive and the North Dallas Tollway, Beckert Park is surrounded by the high-rises of North Dallas. The park is energetic and features an outdoor summer series with jazz, salsa and symphony music.

CONNEMARA MEADOW PRESERVE
North/Allen
300 Tatum Road, Allen
214.351.0990
www.connermaraconservancy.org
Free

The Connemara Meadow Preserve is a beautiful, rich floral land that was set aside by Frances William and her daughter, Amy Monier. Concerned that their family's farmland would be overtaken by urban sprawl, they donated seventy-two acres as one of the first land trusts in Texas. The land is now owned and maintained by the Connemara Conservancy Foundation, a land conservation and environmental education organization.

Members of the conservancy can enjoy an area that is reminiscent of the blackland prairie. Nonmembers are invited to access via a trail at Suncreek Park in Allen and can partake in special events open to the public. One such event is called Into the Meadow; held annually each September, the fundraising event provides an elegant outdoor dining experience featuring local food.

DALLAS ARBORETUM AND BOTANICAL GARDENS
East/White Rock Lake
8525 Garland Road
214.515.6500
www.dallasarboretum.org
Admission charge

The Dallas Arboretum and Botanical Gardens (DABS) is along the eastern shores of White Rock Lake and provides spectacular views of downtown Dallas. The sixty-six-acre grounds are a combination of the Rancho Encinal estate and the Alex and Roberta Coke Camp estate.

The forty-four-acre Rancho Encinal was built for geophysicist Everette Lee DeGolyer and his wife, Nell. The Spanish-style DeGolyer house was completed in 1940 and included an extensive four-and-a-half-acre garden. Many of the original garden features remain today, and the home, which is listed in the National Register of Historic Places, is open daily for tours.

Ironically, some sixty years prior to the opening of DABS, Everette DeGolyer was on a committee to find land for a possible arboretum in Dallas. When Nell passed away in 1972, Rancho Encinal was donated to Southern Methodist University (SMU), and the estate was later purchased by the City of Dallas, which designated it as a public park managed by the DABS.

The Alex and Roberta Coke Camp estate, which is adjacent to Rancho Encinal, includes twenty-two acres and an 8,500-square-foot home completed in 1938. The home was designed by well-known architect John Staub and includes Latin, English and French influences. In 1980, DABS raised over $1 million to purchase the home and land.

The combined estates first opened to the public as a botanical garden in 1984, and today, DABS is listed as one of the top arboretums in the world and is home to the internationally acclaimed Rory Meyers Children's Adventure Garden. There are nineteen named gardens providing vibrant displays of color for every season. Annual events, educational programs and family-oriented activities are offered year-round.

Dragon Park
Uptown
3520 Cedar Springs Road
Free

Dragon Park is a very small, tranquil park with beautiful foliage and unique statues, including an eclectic mix of Buddha heads, angels, fairies, gargoyles and—of course—dragons.

Farmers Branch (A City in a Park)
Northeast/Farmers Branch
Farmers Branch Historical Park: 2540 Farmers Branch Lane, Farmers Branch
Keenan Cemetery: 2570 Valley View Lane, Farmers Branch
972.247.3131
www.visitfarmersbranch.com
Free

Located just northeast of Dallas off of Interstate 635, Farmers Branch was once the location of the first settlement in the area. The Peters Colony chose the area due to the fertile soil, wildlife and proximity to water. In 1986, the city founded the Farmers Branch Historical Park to preserve this heritage. The park includes the 1856 Gilbert House, the oldest stone home in Dallas County, which is still standing on its original foundation. Numerous other structures have been moved to the park, including an 1877 depot and 1900 schoolhouse.

The town of Farmers Branch has rightfully earned its nickname, A City in a Park. The small town offers a living history museum, a community garden and thirty award-winning parks, most of which line Rawhide Creek. Be sure to visit the John F. Burke Nature Preserve on Valley View Lane, which has walking trails through two different ecosystems—part wetland and part upland forest. Rawhide Park, located next to the Manske Library, offers a great jogging path with exercise stations and an excellent Old West playground.

Plan a visit in spring or fall, as Farmers Branch has over 500 different varieties and 1,500 rose plants in multiple rose gardens that connect through trails around and near city hall. The Farmers Branch EarthKind and Display Rose Garden off Valley View Lane is also near the Keenan Cemetery. It was established in 1842, when Thomas and Sarah Keenan, of the Peters Colony, buried their son John at the site. It is thought to be the oldest cemetery in Dallas County.

Located just northeast of Dallas, Farmers Branch was home to many of the first settlers in the Peters Colony. Original buildings and reconstructions can be explored at the Historical Park in Farmers Branch. *Photograph by the author.*

Grapevine Springs Preserve
North/Coppell
345 West Bethel Road, Coppell
972.462.5100
www.dallascounty.org
Free

The land where Grapevine Springs Preserve is located has a lasting Texas legacy. It was on this land that Sam Houston camped while he was negotiating a peace treaty with local Native Americans in 1843. In 1936, the Works Progress Administration turned the land into a public park. Today, the sixteen-acre preserve includes a rock-lined channel, bridges and great walking paths.

Griggs Park

Uptown
3200 Colby Street
www.dallasparks.org
Free

Griggs Park was created in 1915 solely for African Americans and originally named the Hall Street Negro Park. In 2013, the park was redeveloped, and a monument honoring Reverend Allen Griggs, for whom the park was renamed, was added.

Reverend Griggs was a former slave who was brought to Texas at age nine. At age twenty-four, he was ordained as a missionary with the Baptist church and served as a minister for most of his life. He was very influential in developing educational opportunities for black Texans and is credited with establishing Texas's first black newspaper.

The seven-and-a-half-acre park is located in Uptown Dallas in the State-Thomas neighborhood. The park includes benches along winding trails that offer excellent views of downtown Dallas.

Katy Trail

Uptown and Highland Park
www.katytraildallas.org
Free

The Southern Branch of the Union Pacific Railroad was established in 1865. The Kansas-Texas route was commonly called K-T (eventually, it was referred to as the Katy). In 1993, Union Pacific donated the abandoned lines to the City of Dallas. Original plans were to use it as part of DART, but locals proposed it be turned into a greenbelt.

In 2000, the Katy Trail opened. The urban trail is set above street traffic and is highly prized by locals and visitors alike. The wide path runs through Uptown and Highland Park, with excellent opportunities to take in amazing views of Dallas. The three-and-a-half-mile trail has multiple access points, with additional extensions planned in the near future. The best places to park are (for access on the north end) Knox Street and (on the southern end) Reverchon Park.

Kidd Springs Park

Oak Cliff
700 West Canty Street
214.670.7535
www.dallasparks.org
Free

Located in Oak Cliff and just north of Bishop Arts District, Kidd Springs Park became part of Dallas Parks and Recreation in 1947. The park includes a large spring-fed lake, where many Dallas residents first learned to swim. Today, the park offers a pool, playgrounds, garden areas, public art and an excellent recreational center.

Kiest Park

Oak Cliff
3080 South Hampton Road
214.670.1918
www.dallasparks.org
Free

Edwin J. Kiest was the owner and publisher of the *Dallas Daily Times Herald*, served as president of the State Fair of Texas from 1908 to 1911 and 1920 to 1921 and served as president of the Dallas City Park Board from 1931 to 1935. His wife, Elizabeth Patterson Lyon Kiest, helped found the Dallas Arts Association. Upon Elizabeth's passing, Edwin donated a large tract of land to the City of Dallas in her memory.

The City of Dallas established the land as Kiest Park in 1930. The 263-acre metropolitan park is located in South Dallas, east of the Oak Cliff Nature Preserve. The park includes a nice 2.8-mile paved trail that meanders through the park, clinging to the edges, with stops at playgrounds, athletic fields, formal gardens, picnic areas and a large recreation center. Access to the park is provided via Kiest Boulevard, Rugged Drive and South Hampton Road.

Klyde Warren Park

Uptown/Downtown
2012 Woodall Rogers Freeway
.214.716.4500
www.klydewarrenpark.org
Free

Klyde Warren Park has helped create a more walkable city by connecting the downtown Dallas Arts District with uptown Dallas. The urban green space was built over the recessed Woodall Rodgers Freeway between Pearl and St. Paul Streets. The 5.2-acre park is a highly active space, with free public programming that includes outdoor concerts, film showings, yoga, a lecture series and more.

The park includes multiple pavilions, shaded seating and a large center great lawn. The far northeast corner includes a children's park with interactive fountains and playgrounds. West of the children's park is the *Dallas Morning News* Reading and Game Room, which includes a lending library and games like checkers, backgammon and chess. A small dog park is located on the far east side, providing a fenced area for off-leash play. A wide granite pathway lined with red oaks and wooden benches surrounds the park. The eastbound and westbound Woodall Rodgers Freeway access streets that border the park are often lined with a variety of food trucks serving up many delicious offerings.

Lake Cliff Park

Oak Cliff
300 East Colorado Boulevard
www.dallasparks.org
Free

On July 4, 1906, an amusement park dubbed "the Southwest's greatest playground" was opened by local entrepreneurs in Oak Cliff. It contained a giant pool, waterslides, a skating rink and theaters. After a few years of financial troubles, the owners sold most of the land to the City of Dallas in 1914.

George Kessler, designer of Fair Park, developed a master plan for the forty-five-acre park. The original swimming pool from the amusement park became Dallas's first municipal pool, and a bathhouse was opened in 1921.

Other projects, like a formal rose garden and stone pergola, were installed with help from the Work Projects Administration.

The park has gone though many transitions over the years. It remains a beloved green space, with baseball fields, playgrounds, gardens and picnic areas surrounding the sunken freshwater lake.

-

LAKESIDE PARK
North/Highland Park
4601 Lakeside Drive, Highland Park
www.hptx.org
Free

The municipality of Highland Park is located a few miles north of downtown Dallas and is well-known for its multimillion-dollar homes and famous residents. The main road, Lakeside Drive, runs parallel with Turtle Creek, a tributary of the Trinity River. Alongside the creek is a fourteen-acre swath of green space that is immaculately landscaped.

You will feel transported into a world of wealth and decadence when strolling through the park and watching swans swim in the creek. Be sure to make it to the northern side to Turtle Creek Dam and cross the bridge to see the whimsical teddy bear statues. On the southern side of the park and past Armstrong Avenue, you can connect to the Turtle Creek Greenbelt Trail that winds through Oak Lawn and Reverchon Parks.

MOORE PARK
South
1900 East Eighth Street
www.dallasparks.org
Free

Moore Park was created in 1938 after the Oak Cliff Civic League petitioned the city for a new park. Originally named the Eighth Street Negro Park, it was renamed for Will Moore, a community activist with the National Association for the Advancement of Colored People (NAACP). It was rededicated during a 1940 Juneteenth celebration. Created at a time when harassment and government-sanctioned rules kept African Americans from going to "white" parks, it became a gathering place for the black community.

Cedar Creek runs through the park to its mouth at the Trinity River. A new bridge was recently added that connects the park to the Santa Fe Trestle Trail. The 24.6-acre park includes sports fields, playground, trails, picnic areas, an excellent twenty-five-foot overlook and an elevated walkway to a terraced grove of oak trees.

Oak Lawn Park

Uptown
3333 Turtle Creek Boulevard
214.526.7664
www.dallasparks.org
Free

Oak Lawn Park is an immaculate twenty-acre park at the Uptown and Oak Lawn intersection with connections to Turtle Creek Trail. The City of Dallas bought the land and officially established it as a park in 1909. Prior to this purchase, the Dallas Consolidated Electric Street Railway owned the land, and it was used as a green gathering space with backing from developers who were promoting Dallas's first northern suburbs.

In 1936, the city added a statue of Robert E. Lee to the park and changed the name to Robert E. Lee Park. In 2017, following community pressure to ensure everyone feels welcome and safe, the Dallas Park Board removed the statue of Lee and renamed the park Oak Lawn Park.

Pike Park

Uptown
2807 Harry Hines Boulevard
www.dallasparks.org
Free

Pike Park is a 4.3-acre community park that was established in 1915 in what was then known as Little Mexico. Little Mexico was a permanent settlement for many Mexico-born migrants who came to Dallas to work on the railroad system. The park, originally called Summit Play Park, included a Mission-style recreation center that was designed by Lang & Witchell, prominent Dallas builders of the time.

Pike Park was established in 1915 in what was then known as Little Mexico, a permanent settlement for many Mexico-born migrant workers. *Photograph by the author.*

The recreation center has been renovated but has kept most of the original style. In 2000, the City of Dallas added Pike Park to its Dallas Landmark listings in an attempt to preserve the park and increase awareness of the heritage of the neighborhood. Today, the park includes a recreation center, baseball fields, basketball courts, a pavilion and a playground.

Pleasant Oaks Park
Southeast
8701 Greenmound Avenue
214.670.0941
www.dallasparks.org
Free

Enjoy a full day of activities at Pleasant Oaks Park. The 18.7-acre community park and recreation center offers swimming, tennis courts and playgrounds. Pleasant Oaks Park was established in 1952 and is flanked by large oak trees.

Reverchon Park
North of Victory Park/West of Uptown
Maple Avenue and Turtle Creek Boulevard
3505 Maple Avenue
214.670.7721
www.reverchonparkfriends.com
Free

Reverchon Park, like many other large urban parks, has been through many transitions. It is currently a forty-six-acre park that ties to the Katy Trail and has beautiful grounds with gardens, pavilions and baseball fields.

When Dallas purchased the land in 1915, it was known as Woodchuck Hill, a dangerous makeshift slum filled with people squatting on the land and living in makeshift houses and tents. After the City of Dallas made the $40,000 land purchase, the city began to clear the land and create a city park, which it temporarily named Turtle Creek Park after the Turtle Creek tributary of the Trinity River, which bounds part of the park.

Soon after, the park was renamed after Julien Reverchon. Reverchon was born in France but moved to Dallas in 1856 as part of the La Reunion community. In Dallas, he became a well-known botanist who collected native plants. By the time of his death, he had amassed a herbarium of over twenty thousand specimens.

In the 1920s, people traveled from all over Texas to the park to get water from the Gill Well, which was thought to provide healing power. When a grandstand and ballpark were added in 1924, the park sealed its place as a civic hot spot. In the 1930s, the Works Progress Administration brought additional improvements, like gardens, picnic areas and playground equipment. In 1951, the city purchased an additional ten acres of land, bringing the park total to forty-six acres.

In the 1980s and early 1990s, a lack of city funding and maintenance led to the beloved park turning into a place for criminals and addicts. In 1998, major efforts by volunteers and the city took back the park. Soon after, the Friends of Reverchon Park was established to help unify support of the park, and it has once again become a cherished city park.

Trinity River Audubon Center
Southeast
6500 Great Trinity Forest Way (formerly South Loop 12)
214.398.8722
www.trinityriver.audubon.org
Admission charge

The Trinity River Audubon Center is part of the National Audubon Society, a nonprofit organization that helps protect birds and educate students about science, conservation and ecosystems. The center is located about ten miles southeast of downtown on land that was formerly an illegal landfill. Through the 1980s and 1990s, over two million cubic yards of trash were illegally dumped at the Deepwood site.

Residents of the nearby Pleasant Groove and Shady Hills neighborhoods fought to stop the dumping for over twenty years, all while continuing to endure health impacts due to the pollution. In a precedent-setting environmental law case, U.S. District Judge Barefoot Sanders ruled that the City of Dallas contributed to the illegal dumping by doing nothing to stop the activity and bore the responsibility to clean up the site. In 2003, an agreement was made to turn the remediated landfills into part of the Trinity River Project and open a nature center at the site.

The Trinity River Audubon Center opened in 2008, truly turning trash into treasure. The center is the gateway to exploring the six-thousand-acre Great Trinity Forest, which is the largest hardwood bottomland urban forest in the United States. It supports a variety of plant and animal species, including over sixty resident bird species and two hundred migrant species that pass through on the journey between Canada and Mexico.

Enjoy five miles of nature viewing trails, almost all of which are wheelchair-accessible. A trail map is available on the website and in the center. The trails explore three ecosystems: wetlands, forest and prairie. In addition to the birds, you will be able to see beehives and enjoy the butterfly garden.

The ecofriendly center, designed by Antoine Predock, was created to minimize environmental impact as well as repair some of the preexisting problems at the site. At the center, you can watch movies, take a conservation class, enjoy a workshop or visit the indoor exhibit hall featuring native animals. Unique and locally made gifts are available at the Nature Store.

Trinity River Greenbelt and Great Trinity Forest
Along the Trinity River, West of Downtown
Trammel Crow Park: 3700 Sylvan Avenue
Continental Avenue Bridge and West Dallas Gateway: 109 Continental Avenue
Trinity Overlook: 110 West Commerce Street
Texas Horse Park: 811 Pemberton Hill Road
MoneyGram Soccer Park: 2200 Walnut Hill Lane
William Blair Jr. Park: 3000 Rochester Street
Big Spring Site: 1121 Pemberton Hill Road
www.trinityrivercorridor.com
Free

The 710-mile Trinity River is the longest watershed entirely within the state of Texas. As the West Fork and Elm Fork merge in Dallas, they form the Trinity River. Dallas has experienced disastrous flooding from the Trinity, and the Trinity River Corridor Project aims to transform the city's flood zone into a large urban park.

The project is well underway, with beautiful bridges designed by architect Santiago Calatrava. Multiple parks have opened, including the Trammel Crow Park, MoneyGram Soccer Park and the Texas Horse Park. From the Trammel Crow Park, one can see spectacular views of downtown and access the Trinity Skyline Trail and Trinity Levee Top Loop Trail.

The Trinity River Project is not just about parks. First and foremost, it is about safety and is designed to protect Dallas and its residents from flooding. It is also about the environment and is meant to restore and preserve ecological resources in Dallas. There are more than ten thousand acres in the project area, with a wide variety of ecosystems.

Along the Trinity River is the Great Trinity Forest. It is thought to be the largest urban bottomland hardwood forest in America and the largest forest within any city limits. The forest contains multiple chains of wetlands and 1,410 acres of grassland, 4,677 acres of forest land and 1,001 acres of management stands. There are also large green spaces for the public's enjoyment, such as the nine-hundred-acre William Blair Jr. Park. Additionally, the Big Spring Site received designation as a Dallas Landmark in 2016. Big Spring, a 15.42-acre land tract that includes one of the last intact springs in the area, is part of the land claimed by early Dallas pioneer John Beeman.

Trinity River Expeditions
214.941.1757
www.canoedallas.com
Rental charge

Trinity River Expeditions provides equipment, transportation and information to help people explore hundreds of miles along the Upper Trinity Basin. Due to the periodic flooding of the Trinity River, there are plenty of undeveloped areas along the river. A canoe trip on the river can provide access to historic bridges, mill sites and ferries.

Turtle Creek Greenbelt Trail
Highland Park to Oak Lawn
4700 Drexel Drive
Free

Turtle Creek Greenbelt is a two-mile-long walking trail popular with dog walkers. It meanders through Highland Park to Oak Lawn and has connection points to Katy Trail at Oak Lawn and Reverchon Parks.

White Rock Lake
Northeast
8100 Doran Circle
214.670.8740
www.whiterocklake.org
Free

The 1,015 acres currently home to White Rock Lake Park were originally part of a bison-hunting ground for Native Americans. In the 1840s, after the Native Americans were forced out of the area, the land became farmland for the Daniel and Cox families. The land took another turn in the early 1900s, when the fast-growing city of Dallas was experiencing a water shortage. Construction started in 1910 to create a reservoir by damming White Rock Creek. Soon after water started to pump from White Rock Lake, the people of Dallas realized the reservoir would not keep up with the demand. Construction for Lake Lewisville started, and White Rock Lake stopped being a source of water in 1929.

The Bath House and White Rock Lake. *Courtesy of Donna Kidby.*

As White Rock Lake shifted from being a water source, the people of Dallas realized the area was perfect for outdoor recreation. On December 13, 1929, White Rock Lake and the surrounding land officially became a city park.

The Civilian Conservation Corps (CCC) had a camp at White Rock Lake and provided training and education to young men from 1935 to 1942. A statue at the park honors the CCC workers and their efforts at the park, including planting 1,500 trees and constructing overlooks, pavilions and recreation buildings.

The first permanent lakeside amenities were the Bath House and Bathing Beach on the eastern shore. Swimming at the lake was very popular but was banned in 1952. Today, the Bath House serves as a cultural center and includes the White Rock Lake Museum. The museum opened in 2004 and provides information on the park's natural and cultural history.

White Rock Lake now includes over nine miles of hike/bike trails, rental facilities, boat ramps, a dog park, birdwatching areas and excellent playgrounds. Motorized boats are not allowed. It is a wonderful spot to kayak and sail. Parking for the lake and surrounding parks is available off Buckner Boulevard, Mockingbird Lane and West Lawther Drive. The sixty-six-acre Dallas Arboretum and Botanical Gardens is located off the southeast shores, with parking and entrances on Garland Road. An admission fee is required at the Dallas Arboretum and Botanical Gardens.

8

THEY CAME TO PLAY

Sports are a significant and thriving part of the culture in Dallas. In fact, *Sporting News* recently awarded Dallas with the distinction of being a "Best Sports City." As home to six major sports teams, many additional minor-league teams and a thriving collegiate sports presence and fanbase, the Dallas metropolitan area offers great opportunities for people to enjoy a variety of sporting events. All of these options also continue to spur the growth of the city and attract visitors and tourists.

It was the growth of the city that enabled Dallas to attract professional sports teams. Just as railroads expanded business, they also facilitated the spread of sports to the southern states. Prior to World War II, most professional sports teams were in the northern United States, with teams connected by daylong train rides. Los Angeles was the first city in the West to get a major-league football franchise when the Cleveland Rams moved to California in 1945. Dallas did not follow until fifteen years later, when the city was granted a National Football League (NFL) franchise, and the Dallas Cowboys, "America's Team," made their debut.

Dallas has claimed elite status in many ways, not least with football. What may be considered the most elite professional sports game and the biggest advertising event of the year, the Super Bowl, was named by Dallas resident Lamar Hunt. The Dallas Cowboys, currently the most valuable sports franchise in the United States, are one of the few professional football teams to have won three Super Bowl titles.

The first Cotton Bowl was played in 1937 and was financed by J. Curtiss Sandford, a Texas oil tycoon. The Cotton Bowl stadium, located in Fair Park, was also the first home of the Dallas Cowboys. *Photograph by the author.*

Even though the Dallas Cowboys did not arrive until 1960, Dallas has a long football history. The Cotton Bowl has been played in Dallas annually since January 1, 1937. J. Curtis Sandford, a Texas oil tycoon, financed the first Cotton Bowl out of his own pocket. This college football championship game was held at the Cotton Bowl stadium in Fair Park from 1937 until 2010, at which point it moved to the AT&T Stadium in Arlington. The Dallas Cowboys also played at the Cotton Bowl stadium from 1960 to 1971. This iconic stadium still hosts a variety of collegiate games and other sporting events.

Although Texas is generally thought of as Football Country, baseball has a long history in the state. In the north, baseball was referred to as the national game by the mid-1850s. As early as 1861, an amateur baseball club had started in Houston. As a popular pastime during the Civil War, baseball quickly spread throughout the state. A professional minor league, the Texas League, was established in 1888, and several Texas cities strived to participate in the league. Investors secured Dallas's entry to the league by raising the funds to attract fine players and create a new ballpark in suburban Oak Cliff. The creation of the Dallas Hams drew large crowds, and the team won two league titles in 1888. Although the Texas League collapsed due to lack of funds, Dallas continued to dominate the games in a new combined league, the Texas-Southern.

In addition to the interesting name, the minor-league Dallas Hams took on other names through the team's history, including Dallas Navigators (1896), Braves (1902), Submarines (1917–18), Marines (1919–22) and Rebels (1939–42). Possibly offering foresight into the major league team to come, the minor-league team was also named the Rangers in 1958.

When the major-league baseball team the Washington Senators moved to the Dallas–Fort Worth area in 1972, the team was eagerly welcomed by local baseball fans. The Texas Rangers finished last in 1972 and 1973 but experienced their first winning season in 1974, when the team finished with an 84–76 record and in second place in the American League West. The Rangers have appeared in the MLB postseason eight times and have many players who have been inducted into the Texas Sports Hall of Fame, including Nolan Ryan, the first pitcher to get five thousand strikeouts (in 1989).

Dallas is also well-known for its professional basketball teams. The YMCA and the army played major roles in spreading the game throughout the Unites States and the world after it was created in the late nineteenth century. Local leagues and small championships were common in the early twentieth century. In addition, many colleges adopted the sport.

In 1949, the National Basketball League and the Basketball Association of America merged and formed the National Basketball Association (NBA). The NBA became the significant force for professional basketball expansion. Professional basketball made its way to Dallas in 1980, when the NBA approved a new franchise. Excited fans chose the name, the Mavericks, based on the 1950s television Western *Maverick*. The Dallas Mavericks, often referred to as the Mavs, have set the record for the longest consecutive sellout streak in the United States. The team has won three division titles, two conference championships and the 2011 NBA Championship.

Women's basketball developed in tandem with men's basketball, with early adopters learning of the sport through affiliation with the YMCA. The first women's collegiate basketball game was played between Stanford University and the University of California, Berkeley, in 1896. The sport's popularity spread for decades. The NBA founded the Women's National Basketball Association (WNBA) in 1996. There are currently twelve teams in the WNBA, including the Dallas Wings.

Hockey came to Dallas in 1993, when the Minnesota North Stars relocated and became the Dallas Stars. Contemporary hockey was developed in Canada, with the first indoor game taking place in 1875 at Montreal's Victoria Skating Rink. By 1893, the first match in the United States was held between Yale University and Johns Hopkins University. The National Hockey League was formed in 1917 and expanded into the United States in 1924 with the addition of the Boston Bruins. Hockey was incredibly popular in the northern United States, but it was not until the 1990s that the league started an ambitious plan to focus on expansion in southern states. In 1999, the Dallas Stars won the Stanley Cup, the oldest existing trophy awarded through a professional sports franchise.

It can be hard to imagine hockey as a popular sport in a city that often tops one hundred degrees in the summer months. The Texas Rangers have had similar struggles with setting records for the hottest games in MLB history. Although the heat can impact sports, the culture is there. The southern states, coined "Sun Belt States," experienced massive population migration in the 1970s. As people migrated from northern states, they brought their passion for their northern sports. The economic shifts due to oil booms and big business movements also impacted investments in sports in the South. Sports is big business, and it is no surprise that the economic powerhouse of Dallas is also home to powerhouses in sports.

YOUR GUIDE TO HISTORY

Fretz Park soccer champions of 1928. *Courtesy of Dallas Municipal Archives.*

DALLAS COWBOYS (NFL)
Far West/Arlington
AT&T Stadium
One AT&T Way, Arlington
817.892.4000
www.dallascowboys.com

Originally known as the Steers and then the Dallas Rangers, the team did not take on the name Cowboys until 1960, soon after Dallas was granted an NFL franchise. In the 1960s, the new NFL team played home games at the Cotton Bowl located in Fair Park. It wasn't until 1966 that the Cowboys posted the team's first winning season. Although the Cowboys were defeated in the postseason, 1966 became a pivotal turning point for postseason appearances by the team.

In 1970, the team made its first Super Bowl appearance, and the following season, the Cowboys moved to a new stadium in Irving, a suburb of Dallas. The Cowboys won their first Super Bowl in 1971, and the team's popularity continued to grow throughout the 1970s as they started to receive more nationwide attention, including after the introduction of the first modern cheerleading squad. The team won its second Super Bowl in 1977.

The 1980s were not as friendly to the team, with some of the seasons dominated by criticism, change and controversy. New management and skillful drafts brought the Cowboys back into the fold of the NFL elite by the 1990s, a decade when the team won three Super Bowls (in 1992, 1993 and 1995).

In 2009, the team moved to a new stadium, the AT&T Stadium in Arlington. Jerry Jones, the owner of the Dallas Cowboys, envisioned it an entertainment mecca, and it is one of the largest stadiums in the NFL. The stadium is not just home to the Dallas Cowboys but has also hosted concerts and other sports tournaments. Self-guided and art tours of the stadium are available.

DALLAS MAVERICKS BASKETBALL CLUB (NBA)
Victory Park/American Airlines Center
2500 Victory Avenue
214.222.9687
www.nba.com/mavericks

The Dallas Mavericks are named after the 1950s television Western *Maverick*. Fans chose the name soon after the 1980 vote to admit a new

NBA franchise for Dallas. Since the team's inception, the Mavs have won two conference championships, three division titles, and one NBA championship (2010–2011 season). The team plays home games at the American Airlines Center. Check the site for the schedule and watch for promotional and giveaway nights.

DALLAS POLO CLUB
Far South/Red Oak
730 Bent Trail, Red Oak
214.979.0300
www.dallaspoloclub.org

The Dallas Polo Club is located at the Bear Creek Polo Ranch, about thirty minutes south of Dallas. The outdoor season starts in April and runs through mid-November. Matches are held in an indoor arena through winter and early spring. There is usually at least one polo match per month that is open to the public, and schedules can be found online.

DALLAS RATTLERS (MLL)
Far North/Frisco
Ford Center at The Star
One Cowboys Way, Frisco
www.dallasrattlers.com

The Dallas Rattlers are a Major League Lacrosse (MLL) team that moved from Rochester, New York, to Texas in 2018. The team plays home games at the Ford Center at the Star in Frisco.

DALLAS STARS HOCKEY CLUB (NHL)
Victory Park/American Airlines Center
2500 Victory Avenue
214.467.8277
stars.nhl.com

Founded in 1967 as the Minnesota North Stars, this franchise relocated to Dallas in 1993. As part of the National Hockey League (NHL), the team has won multiple division titles, the Western Conference championship and the Stanley Cup (in 1998 and 1999). The team plays home games at the American Airlines Center. While you are checking out the game dates for the Dallas Stars, be sure to take a look at the Dallas Stars Foundation, and if you want to hit the ice, there are multiple Star Center Rinks throughout the Dallas suburbs.

Dallas Wings (WNBA)
Far West/Arlington
College Park Center/University of Texas at Arlington
600 South Center Street, Arlington
wings.wnba.com

The Dallas Wings play in the Western Conference in the Women's National Basketball Association (WNBA). The team started in Detroit, Michigan, as the Detroit Shock in 1998. They were one of the first WNBA expansion teams. The team moved to Tulsa, Oklahoma, in 2010 and were known as the Tulsa Shock. After the team moved to Texas, the name was changed to the Dallas Wings, and the Wings started to play in Arlington at the start of the 2016 WNBA season. The team plays home games at College Park Center at the University of Texas at Arlington. Since its inception, the team has won four Conference Championships and three WNBA Championships. Single-game tickets, season memberships and premium membership information are available on the team's website.

Devil's Bowl Speedway
Far East/Mesquite
1711 Lawson Road, Mesquite
972.222.2421
www.devilsbowl.com

Devil's Bowl Speedway is located in Mesquite, about fifteen miles east of downtown Dallas. From mid-March through October, dirt track races are held every Saturday night.

FC Dallas Soccer Club (MLS)
Far North/Frisco
Toyota Stadium
9200 World Cup Way, Frisco
469.365.0000
www.fcdallas.com

The FC Dallas Soccer Club is based in Frisco, a northern suburb of Dallas. The team was founded in 1995 and competes as a member of Major League Soccer. The team plays at the Toyota Stadium and Toyota Soccer Center, a top venue for pro and amateur soccer.

Frisco Rough Riders (MiLB)
Far North/Frisco
Dr. Pepper Ballpark
7300 Rough Riders Trail, Frisco
972.731.9200
www.milb.com

The Rough Riders, an official Minor League Baseball (MiLB) team, play at the Dr. Pepper Ballpark in Frisco, a northern suburb of Dallas. Check the schedule online for discounts and behind-the-scenes tours of the ballpark.

Lone Star Park at Grand Prairie
Far West/Grand Prairie
1000 Lone Star Parkway, Grand Prairie
972.263.RACE

Located about twenty minutes west of Downtown Dallas in Grand Prairie, Lone Star Park is a Class I racetrack. There are two live racing seasons. Thoroughbred racing starts in April, and quarter-horse racing starts in September. The first race was held in 1997, and since then, Lone Star Park has continued to be a favorite destination for racing enthusiasts. There are various fine dining and bar options at the track, and private suites are available for rent. Check the online calendar for race details. On select nights, visitors can enjoy a free concert with the price of general admission.

Mesquite Championship Rodeo
Fat East/Mesquite
Mesquite Arena
1818 Rodeo Drive, Mesquite
972.285.8777
www.mesquiterodeo.com

The professional rodeo comes to Mesquite, Texas, between June and August. Watch bareback riding, steer wrestling, roping and racing with thousands of other guests. Tickets available through Ticketmaster or by calling the arena. Admission varies by seat and event.

Texas Airhogs
Far West/Grand Prairie
1600 Lone Star Parkway, Grand Prairie
972.521.6730
www.airhogsbaseball.com

The Texas Airhogs started in 2008 and are part of the American Association of Independent Professional Baseball. The team pays at Airhogs Stadium, located about twenty minutes west of Downtown Dallas in Grand Prairie.

Texas Rangers (MLB)
Far West/Arlington
Globe Life Park
1000 Ballpark Way, Arlington
817.273.5222
texas.rangers.mlb.com

The Texas Rangers first played an official game in Texas on April 15, 1972. As part of the American League West division, the Rangers have won multiple AL West championships and played in multiple World Series.

The team plays at the Globe Life Park in Arlington, about a twenty-minute trip from downtown Dallas (depending on traffic). Check the schedule and purchase tickets online. Watch for special events, such as postgame fireworks shows or concerts. Ballpark tours are available throughout the year and include a behind-the-scenes look at the batting cages, press box, dugout and more.

9

VISITOR INFORMATION AND RESOURCES

IMPORTANT NUMBERS

Emergencies: 911
Texas Poison Center Network: 1.800.222.1222

TRANSPORTATION INFORMATION

DALLAS AREA RAPID TRANSIT (DART)
214.979.1111
www.dart.org

DART provides public transportation (buses and trains) in Dallas, Carrollton, Farmers Branch, Garland, Irving, Plano and Richardson and has a Fort Worth and Denton County line.

Statue at Fair Park, a 277-acre park with over thirty art deco structures built for the Texas Centennial Exposition. *Courtesy of Donna Kidby.*

Dallas is served by two major airports, Dallas Love Field and Dallas/Fort Worth International Airport (DFW). This statue welcomes visitors at Dallas Love Field. *Photograph by the author.*

Texas Department of Transportation
www.dfwtraffic.dot.state.tx.us

Visit the website for information about incidents, lane closures and rail routes.

North Texas Tollway Authority (NTTA)
www.ntta.org

All tolls in Dallas are cashless. Cars are scanned for a toll tag, which deducts the toll from a user's account. If a vehicle does not have a toll tag, a ZipCash bill will be sent to the owner based on vehicle registration records. ZipCash is a premium charge over toll-tag pricing. If renting a car, ask the rental agency about its toll tag policy.

Major Airports

Dallas Love Field
8008 Herb Kelleher Way
214.670.6080
dallas-lovefield.com

Dallas/Fort Worth International Airport (DFW)
2400 Aviation Drive
972.973.3112
dfw.airport.com

Dallas is served by two major airports, Dallas Love Field (DAL) and Dallas/Fort Worth International Airport (DFW). DAL is closer to downtown, with only a fifteen-minute commute during slow traffic periods. However, DFW is larger and may offer more flight options.

Statues located in the Founders' Plaza Plane Observation Area at Dallas/Fort Worth International Airport (DFW). *Photograph by the author.*

Plan for a minimum commute of forty minutes to DFW if traveling from downtown (or more time during peak traffic periods). When flying out of DFW, be sure to check the terminal, as the airport spans over twenty-nine square miles. In addition, visitors should note that entering and exiting the airport requires a TollTag or payment of a toll—even for drop-off and pickup purposes.

If you have time, stop by Founders' Plaza at DFW (1700 North Airfield Drive). The plaza includes telescopes, broadcasts of the control tower operators, commemorative monuments and statues.

Visitor Information

City of Dallas Office of Cultural Affairs (OCA)
www.dallasculture.org

The City of Dallas Office of Cultural Affairs works to enhance the vitality of the city and the quality of life for all Dallas citizens. Through support

Murals and statues at Fair Park depict the different governments that have ruled over Texas. *Courtesy of Donna Kidby.*

and partnership for the twenty-three city-owned facilities, OCA helps create environments where art and culture thrive. If you are looking for something creative, inspiring or educational, be sure to check the website for current event listings.

DALLAS CONVENTION AND VISITORS BUREAU
325 North St. Paul Street, Suite 700
214.571.1000 / 800.232.5527
www.visitdallas.com

Free visitors' guides, newsletters, an events calendar and hotel listings are available online.

SUGGESTIONS BY AREA

Downtown

Reunion Tower
Founders' Plaza
Dallas Heritage Village at Old City Park
Old Red Museum
Kennedy Memorial
Dealey Plaza and the Grassy Knoll
Sixth Floor Museum
Dallas Holocaust Museum
West End Historic District
Giant eyeball (*Eye*) on Elm Street
Adolphus and Magnolia Hotels on Commerce Street
Neiman Marcus
Thanks-Giving Square
Perot Museum
Majestic Theatre
Pioneer Plaza & Park Cemetery

Dallas Arts District

Crow Collection of Asian Art
Nasher Sculpture Center
Dallas Museum of Art
Klyde Warren Park
Winspear Opera House
Booker T. Washington High School
St. Paul United Methodist Church
Wyly Theatre
Dallas Symphony Meyerson
Cathedral Santuario de Guadalupe
Belo Mansion

Uptown

Dragon Park
Freedman's Cemetery
Harwood Street Historic District
Samurai Collection
Museum of Geometric and MADI Art
Reverchon Park
Katy Trail
Pike Park
Lakeside Park

East, Northeast and Park Cities

White Rock Lake
Bath House Cultural Center
Lakewood Theatre
Knox/Henderson Historic Neighborhood
Frontiers of Flight Museum
Junius Heights Historic District
Swiss Avenue and Munger Place Historic Districts
Wilson Block Historic District
Peak's Suburban Addition

Southern Methodist University
Latino Cultural Center
Deep Ellum
Fair Park
African American Museum
Music Hall at Fair Park
Dallas Firefighter's Museum
Juanita Craft Civil Rights House

Far North Dallas

Bonnie Parker's gravesite (Crown Hill Cemetery)
Farmers Branch Historical Park
Farmers Branch Cemetery (Keenan Cemetery)
Cavanaugh Flight Museum
Railroad Museum (Plano)
Heritage Farmstead Museum (Plano)
Grapevine Vintage Railroad
Southfork Ranch (Parker)

West Dallas

Trammel Crow Park
Margaret Hunt Bridge
Oak Cliff Historical Neighborhood
Texas Theatre
Bishops Arts Theatre Center
Texas Fire Museum

South Dallas

Park Row Historic District (South Boulevard)
Lake Cliff Historic District
Dallas Zoo
Tenth Street Historic District
Bishop Arts District

Fair Park
Dallas Firefighter's Museum
Wheatley Place Historic District
Winnetka Heights Historic District
Trinity River Audubon Center

Seasonal Information

Dallas weather can be a bit unpredictable. Most months have mild temperatures. The highs can reach into the hundreds in the summer and lows can be in the teens during the winter months. However, winter months usually have lows in the forties or fifties, with occasional but light snow occurring in January and February. The city receives the most precipitation in May. Late spring and early summer also bring the possibility of tornadoes.

The State Fair of Texas, the longest-running state fair in the nation, is held each fall at Fair Park. *Photograph by the author.*

Annual Festivals and Activities

Since festival details often change, be sure to research further before making plans.

Spring

Beckert Park in Addison: Summer series featuring outdoor symphonies (addisontexas.net)

Cinco de Mayo Parade and Festival: Parade and cultural festival held downtown (dallascincodemayo.net)

City Arts Festival: Activities and entertainment held annually in Fair Park (cityartsfestival.com)

Cottonwood Art Festival: Semi-annual free event held in Cottonwood Park in Richardson (cottonwoodartfestival.com)

Crow Collection of Asian Art: Celebrate mid-May merriment and learn about holidays and festivals from across the Asian continent (crowcollection.org)

Dallas Arboretum and Botanical Gardens: Visit to experience Dallas Blooms, one of the largest floral festivals in the Southwest (dallasarboretum.org)

Dallas International Guitar Festival: This is the oldest guitar event in the world, with manufacturers, collectors and musicians selling, trading and performing (guitarshow.com)

Deep Ellum Arts Festival: An enormous street festival on six blocks of Main Street in Deep Ellum (deepellumartsfestival.com)

Earth Day Texas: Admission is free for this annual event at Fair Park that raises environmental awareness (earthdaytx.org)

Grapevine Main Street Festival: Festival held along Main Street in Historic Grapevine (grapevinetexas.org)

Grapevine Vintage Railroad: Easter Bunny Train Ride (grapevinetexasusa.com/grapevine-vintage-railroad.com)

Juneteenth Celebrations: The oldest nationally celebrated commemoration of the end of slavery in the United States; look for events at Fair Park (fairpark.org) and community centers throughout Dallas (juneteenth.com)

Mesquite Championship Rodeos: Legendary rodeo experience and the opportunity to see favorite rodeo events (mesquiterodeo.com)

Scarborough Renaissance Festival: Thirty-five acres with over twenty-four stages and more than two hundred unique acts (srfestival.com)

Texas Black Invitational Rodeo: Annual rodeo hosted by the African American Museum (aamdallas.org)

Summer

Dallas Arboretum and Botanical Gardens: Discounts are often available in the summer (dallasarboretum.org)

Dallas Pride Parade: Started in 1972 as a small parade to commemorate the 1969 Stonewall Riots, the Dallas Pride Parade has grown over the years and now includes dozens of performances, events and a Family Pride Zone, a welcoming place for LGBT parents and kids (dallaspride.org)

Dallas Summer Musicals: Check the calendar for an exciting summer season (dallassummermusicals.org)

Dallas Theatre Center: Check the calendar for Neighborhood Nights schedule (dallastheatercenter.org)

Frontiers of Flight: Moon Day offers unique experiments, exhibits and access to the wonderful museum and children's discovery area (flightmuseum.com)

GrapeFest: The largest wine festival in the Southwest also offers children's activities and carnival rides (grapevinetexasusa.com)

Greek Food Festival of Dallas: Food, music, dancing and a designated kids' area (greekfestivalofdallas.com)

Independence Day Celebrations: Celebrate with fireworks, bands and food; many parks and attractions host special events, including Old-Fashioned Fourth at the Dallas Heritage Village (dallasheritagevillage.org), Freedom Fest at Fair Park (fairpark.org), Farmers Branch Independence Day Celebration (farmersbranchtx.gov) and Kaboom Town in Addison (addisontexas.net)

North Texas Food Bank: Hunger Action Month (NTFB.org)

Plano Balloon Festival: Hot-air balloon festival, marathons, food, fireworks and more (planoballoonfest.org)

Taste of Dallas: Culinary festival with art, kids' zone and fireworks (tasteofdallas.org)

Texas Home & Garden Show: Largest home and garden show in Texas (texashomeandgarden.com)

Texas Discovery Gardens: Butterflies and Bugs! annual family festival (txdg.org)

Viva Dallas! Hispanic Expo: Entertainment, art, health services and more are featured in this expo held in the Dallas Market Hall (gdhcc.com)

Fall

Addison Octoberfest: More than seventy thousand visitors come to enjoy German food, music, dancing and entertainment (addisontexas.net)

American Indian and Southwestern Art Market: Live music, art, food and children's activities (indianmarket.net)

Dallas Arboretum and Botanical Gardens: Over fifty thousand pumpkins and squash transform the arboretum for fall; enjoy a hay maze, scavenger hunts and the nationally acclaimed Pumpkin Village (dallasarboretum.org)

Dallas Dance Festival: Annual festival in the Dallas Arts District featuring emerging and upcoming dance companies (dallasdancefestival.com)

Dallas Firefighter's Museum: National Fire Prevention Week (dallasfiremuseum.com)

Farmers Branch: Veterans Day (farmersbranchtx.gov)

Halloween: Enjoy spooky family fun at many of the local attractions, including Halloween Organ Spooktacular with the Dallas Symphony Orchestra (mydso.com), Boo at the Zoo (dallaszoo.com), Halloween Scream Train with the Grapevine Vintage Railroad (grapevinetexasusa.com), Creepy Crawl-o-ween at the Texas Discovery Gardens (txdg.org) and Owl-O-Ween at the Trinity River Audubon Center (trinityriver.audubon.org)

State Fair of Texas: Celebrate Texas agriculture, art, music, education and community while enjoying lots of fried food and rides at one of the largest state fairs in the United States (bigtex.com)

Texas Red Nations Powwow: Explore Native American culture (powwows.com)

Texas Stampede Rodeo: Enjoy the rodeo in Allen (visitallen.com)

Winter

Autorama: Custom car show that pays tribute to innovative workmanship (autorama.com)

Christmas: Celebrate Christmas at many local parks and attractions, including Twelve Days of Christmas at the Dallas Arboretum and Botanical Gardens (dallasarboretum.org), candlelight events at the Dallas Heritage Village (dallasheritagevillage.org), Christmas Boat Parade and Bonfire (joe-pool-lake. org), Farmers Branch Christmas in the Branch (farmersbranchtx.gov) and Dickens of a Christmas in downtown McKinney (mckinneytexas.org)

Cotton Bowl Parade of Bands: Features high school bands from across the nation (cottonbowl.com)

Dallas Holiday Parade: Kick off the holiday season with the huge traditional holiday parade (dallasholidayparade.com)

Dallas Zoo: Enjoy admission at a reduced price through most of the winter months (dallaszoo.com)

Fair Park: New Year's Day Cotton Bowl (fairpark.org)

Galleria Mall: Ice skating around the largest indoor Christmas tree in the nation (galleriadallas.com)

Gaylord Texan Resort & Convention Center: ICE! A winter wonderland with holiday scenes carved out of more than two million pounds of ice (marriot.com)

Grapevine Vintage Railroad: North Pole Express (grapevinetexasusa.com)

Greenville Avenue St. Patrick's Day Parade: This parade started in 1979 and has grown to become the largest St. Patrick's Day parade in the Southwest (greenvilleave.org)

Highland Park: Join the tradition that has been around since 1927 on the first Thursday in December, when the 140-year-old pecan tree is lit with over five thousand lights at the corner of Preston Road and Armstrong Parkway (hptx.org)

KidFilm Festival: A film festival for all ages (usafilmfestival.com)

Martin Luther King Jr. Parade: Marching bands, floats, drill teams and dance troupes commemorate the work and life of Martin Luther King Jr. (dallasblack.com)

Martin Luther King Jr. Day of Service: Check for volunteer opportunities in your community

New Year's Eve: Big D New Year's Eve Party and countdown in Victory Park (bigdnye.com)

North Park Center: See the tradition that started in 1987 and features more than 1,600 feet of track with thirty-five toy trains running through a miniature Dallas (northparkcenter.com)

Nasher Sculpture Center: Check the website for free outdoor concerts and movie showings (nashersculpturecenter.org)

North Texas Irish Festival: Music, food and art celebrating Irish and Celtic heritage (ntif.org)

Out of the Loop Fringe Festival: Ten-day festival packed with dance, music and visual arts in Addison (watertowertheatre.org)

Russian Festival: Festival of music and art at Southern Methodist University (smu.edu)

Sources for Discounts

Blue Star Museums
www.arts.gov/national/blue-star-museums

Many of the museums located in Dallas participate in the Blue Star Museums program. This national program provides discounts or free admission to active-duty military personnel and their families from Memorial Day through Labor Day.

Dallas CityPASS
www.citypass.com/dallas

A Dallas CityPASS can be purchased online and provides discounted admission to some of Dallas's top attractions.

Historic Preservation and Research Resources

Several buildings and neighborhoods in Dallas have been designated as landmarks and/or are listed in the National Register of Historic Places. Many of these treasures have been highlighted in this book. For more information, please visit the following resources.

City of Dallas—Dallas Landmark Historic Districts
214.670.4209
dallascityhall.com

The City of Dallas created its Historic Preservation Division in 1973 and currently oversees over 140 designated landmarks and historic districts containing thousands of structures. The city provides tax incentives when an owner rehabilitates a historic property. In addition to tax incentives, the division provides design guidelines written specifically for each district and manages a Certificate of Appropriateness program that requires application

Hall of State at Fair Park is the home of the Dallas Historical Society, which was established in 1922. *Courtesy of Donna Kidby.*

from those wishing to construct, demolish or alter a structure. Anyone who violates the ordinance can be fined. Violations can be reported by calling 311 or completing a form on the City of Dallas website.

City of Dallas—Municipal Archives
214.670.5270
dallascityhall.com

The Dallas Municipal Archives were established in 1985. The archives contain over two thousand cubic feet of departmental records in a variety of formats, including photographs, maps, architectural design plans and printed material. There is a wide variety of collections, including the Bonnie and Clyde, John F. Kennedy and Dallas Police Department records. The archives are accessible by appointment only.

Dallas Historical Society
Hall of State at Fair Park
3939 Grand Avenue
214.421.4500
dallashistory.org

The Dallas Historical Society is a nonprofit organization dedicated to the preservation of the history of Dallas and Texas. The organization, which was formed in 1922, provides educational programs, lectures, historic tours and exhibits. The society also owns a large collection of historic photographs, maps, books and more, which are available to researchers.

Preservation Dallas
2922 Swiss Avenue
214.821.3290
preservationdallas.org

Preservation Dallas champions initiatives intended to protect the history and culture of neighborhoods and historic buildings throughout the community. Preservation Dallas occupies the Wilson House in the Wilson Block Historic District, a unique community of preserved Victorian and Queen Anne homes that have been converted into office space and provided rent-free to nonprofits through the Meadows Foundation. Visit the website for information on fall architectural tours and lecture opportunities and to download self-guided walking tour brochures for historic neighborhoods.

Dallas Jewish Historical Society
7900 Northaven Road
214.239.7120
djhs.org

The Dallas Jewish Historical Society (DJHS) grew from the Dallas Jewish Archives, which were started by concerned citizens with a desire to preserve local Jewish History. The DJHS collects, preserves and records the history of the Dallas Jewish community and provides educational and research opportunities.

Dallas Mexican American Historical League
P.O. Box 181885, Dallas, TX 75218
dmahl.org

Established in 2008, the Dallas Mexican American Historical League researches, collects and documents the city's Mexican American history. The league provides educational programs and exhibits to educate the public about the contributions of Mexican Americans in Dallas.

Remembering Black Dallas
P.O. Box 764436, Dallas, TX 75376
469.399.6242
rbdallas.com

Remembering Black Dallas is a nonprofit organization that preserves and promotes the African American history, artifacts and culture of Dallas and the surrounding cities. The organization hosts and participates in several events throughout the year, including field trips and summits. Monthly meetings are held at the African American Museum in Fair Park and are open to the public. Visit the website for additional information.

Visitor Bureaus/Centers

Addison
5300 Belt Line Road, Dallas, TX 75234
www.addisontexas.net

Dallas Convention and Visitors Bureau
325 North St. Paul Street, Suite 700, Dallas, TX 75201
214.571.1000/800.232.5527
www.visitdallas.com

Farmers Branch
13000 William Dodson Parkway, Farmers Branch, TX 75234
www.visitfarmersbranch.com

Another view of the *Cattle Drive* sculptures at Pioneer Plaza. *Courtesy of Donna Kidby.*

Fort Worth
111 West Fourth Street, Suite 200, Fort Worth, TX 76102
www.fortworth.com

Frisco
6801 Gaylord Parkway, Suite 401, Frisco, TX 75034
www.visitfrisco.com

Glen Rose
100 NE Barnard Street, Glen Rose, TX 76043
www.glenrosetexas.net

Grapevine
636 South Main Street, Grapevine, TX 76051
www.grapevinetexasusa.com

Mesquite
757 North Galloway Avenue, Mesquite, Texas 75149
www.realtexasflavor.com

Plano
Spring Creek Parkway, Plano, Texas 75074
www.visitplano.com

Richardson
411 West Arapaho Road, Suite 105, Richardson, TX 75080
www.richardsontexas.org

Tyler
315 North Broadway Avenue, Tyler, TX 75702
www.cityoftyler.org

Publications and News

Newspapers

Dallas Morning News
508 Young Street, Dallas, TX 75202
www.dallasnews.com

Dallas Observer
2501 Oak Lawn Avenue, Suite 355, Dallas, TX 75219
www.dallasobserver.com

Dallas Post Tribune
2726 South Beckley Avenue, Dallas, TX 75224
www.dallasposttrib.com

Dallas Weekly
3101 Martin Luther King Jr Blvd, Dallas TX 75215
www.dallasweekly.com

Dallas Voice
1825 Market Center Boulevard, Suite 240, Dallas, TX 75207
www.dallasvoice.com

Magazines

Various publications
www.dfwchild.com

DFWChild is the publisher of award-winning parenting magazines *DallasChild, FortWorthChild, NorthTexasChild, Thrive* and *DallasChildBaby.* Online resources include a great calendar, health and wellness tips, travel articles, party suggestions and information about those with special needs.

D Magazine
www.dmagazine.com

A monthly magazine that features great food, art, style, wellness and travel articles.

Texas Monthly
www.texasmonthly.com

A highly respected monthly publication that features politics, food, travel and culture articles.

Other Links

buildingcommunity**WORKSHOP**
416 South Ervay Street
214.252.2900
www.bcworkshop.org

A Texas-based nonprofit community design center that improves the livability and viability of communities where resources are scarce.

KERA 90.1 FM
www.kera.org

Keep an ear and eye out for the excellent Art&Seek (artandseek.org) and information provided by KERA, an NPR affiliate station in North Texas.

Metroplex Baby and Kids
www.metroplexbaby.com

North Texas Kids
www.northtexaskids.com

Travel Savvy Mom
www.travelsavvymom.com

SELECTED BIBLIOGRAPHY

WEBSITES

The websites for the attractions, festivals, neighborhoods and sports teams listed in this book provide valuable information. Prior to planning a visit, please check websites for any given attraction's current hours, prices, closures or special events and opportunities.

The material provided by the City of Dallas Historic Preservation Division and the Municipal Archives offices (dallascityhall.com), especially the Landmark Designation Reports, provided a wealth of insight into Dallas's Landmark Districts and individual structures.

The Portal to Texas History (texashistory.unt.edu), provided by the University of North Texas and hundreds of partnering contributors, also served as an amazing resource for research and insight. The portal is home to a massive collection of images, text, recordings and manuscript collections.

BOOKS

Acheson, Sam. *Dallas Yesterday*. University Park, TX: Southern Methodist University Press, 1977.
Alexander, Charles. *The Ku Klux Klan in the Southwest*. Lexington: University Press of Kentucky, 1965.

Selected Bibliography

Behnken, Brian D. *Fighting Their Own Battles: Mexican Americans, African Americans, and the Struggle for Civil Rights in Texas.* Chapel Hill: University of North Carolina Press, 2011.

Boswell, Angela. *Women in Texas History.* College Station: Texas A&M University Press, 2018.

Doty, Mark. *Lost Dallas.* Charleston, SC: Arcadia Publishing, 2012.

Govenar, Alan B. *Deep Ellum: The Other Side of Dallas.* College Station: Texas A&M University Press, 2013.

Guinn, Jeff. *Go Down Together: The True, Untold Story of Bonnie and Clyde.* New York: Simon & Schuster, 2009.

Hazel, Michael V. *Dallas.* Austin: Texas State Historical Association, 1997.

Hill, Patricia Evridge. *Dallas: The Making of a Modern City.* Austin: University of Texas Press, 1996.

Manchester, William. *Death of a President.* New York: Harper & Row, 1967.

Phillips, Michael. *White Metropolis.* Austin: University of Texas Press, 2006.

Slate, John H. *Historic Dallas Parks.* Charleston, SC: Arcadia Publishing, 2010.

INDEX

U

University of North Texas (UNT) 92

Uptown 163

V

Vaughan, Stevie Ray 113
Viola Court Apartments 23
visitors bureaus 173

W

Walker, Peter 109
Walker, T-Bone 43, 113
Washington, Booker T. 24
Washington Senators 149
Webb, Isaac 15
West Dallas 164
West End Historic District 49
Western Heights Cemetery 63
Wheatley, Phillis 72
Wheatley Place Historic District 72, 86
White Rock Lake 98, 101, 128, 129, 131, 133, 145, 146
White Rock Lake Museum 102, 146
William, Frances 132
Wilson Block Historic District 50, 172
Wilson, Fredick 50
Wilson, Henrietta 50
Wilson House 50, 172
Winnetka Heights 62, 72
Winspear Opera House 111, 118
Woodall Rodgers Freeway 138
Woodchuck Hill 142
Woodrow Wilson High School 33, 103
Work Projects Administration (WPA) 139

Works Progress Administration (WPA) 41, 135, 142
World War I 54
World War II 55, 59, 71, 103, 147
Wright, Frank Lloyd 119
Wyly Theater 119

Y

Young House 22

ABOUT THE AUTHOR

Georgette Driscoll was born and raised in the historic town of Santa Fe, New Mexico. She grew up with a fascination with Dallas and moved to the Big D for her career with a Fortune 500 company. Her first book, *Are We There Yet? Dallas*, was published in November 2015 by Little Green Apples. Georgette is an avid traveler and shares her adventures and passion for history with her husband, John, and her two extraordinary boys, Jack and Walt.

CPSIA information can be obtained
at www.ICGtesting.com
Printed in the USA
LVHW080812230620
658109LV00035BA/185